Communications
in Computer and Information Science   1436

More information about this series at http://www.springer.com/series/7899

Rajeev Agrawal · Goutam Sanyal ·
Kevin Curran · Valentina Emilia Balas ·
Madhu Sharma Gaur (Eds.)

Cybersecurity in Emerging Digital Era

First International Conference, ICCEDE 2020
Greater Noida, India, October 9–10, 2020
Revised Selected Papers

 Springer

Editors
Rajeev Agrawal (iD)
GL Bajaj Institute of Technology
and Management
Greater Noida, India

Kevin Curran (iD)
University of Ulster
Derry, UK

Madhu Sharma Gaur (iD)
GL Bajaj Institute of Technology
and Management
Greater Noida, India

Goutam Sanyal
National Institute of Technology Durgapur
Durgapur, India

Valentina Emilia Balas (iD)
Aurel Vlaicu University of Arad
Arad, Romania

ISSN 1865-0929   ISSN 1865-0937 (electronic)
Communications in Computer and Information Science
ISBN 978-3-030-84841-5   ISBN 978-3-030-84842-2 (eBook)
https://doi.org/10.1007/978-3-030-84842-2

This Springer imprint is published by the registered company Springer Nature Switzerland AG
The registered company address is: Gewerbestrasse 11, 6330 Cham, Switzerland

Preface

In the present era, our lives are transforming rapidly and things around us are becoming smart, intelligent, and seamlessly connected and communicating in new ways. For technocrats and researchers, the future lies in the emerging technologies and man-machine association. Smart systems, digital applications, and services are growing at a faster rate with their presence in every domain, whether it is public or private. However, this digital transformation is evolving with higher risks which need highly resilient and secure solutions that can adapt to the changes and respond to the constant growth. There are several socioeconomic aspects and integration issues and challenges with these services related to their security, privacy, and authentication assurance.

This book presents selected proceedings of the International Conference on Cybersecurity in Emerging Digital Era (ICCEDE 2020). ICCEDE 2020 was held during October 9–10, 2020, and was organized by the department of Master of Computer Applications (MCA) at the G. L. Bajaj Institute of Technology and Management, India (affiliated to APJ Abdul Kalam Technical University). The conference was conducted online due to the ongoing COVID-19 pandemic.

The aim of ICCEDE 2020 was to bring together vibrant stakeholders who share a passion for research and innovation, including solution development partners, end-users, and budding professionals around the world, to deliberate upon the different challenging aspects and issues in the emerging digital transformation. During the conference, a "Special Youth Session" in association with C-DAC Noida, India, was organized for college students to increase the awareness and basic understanding of concepts surrounding the importance of security and privacy in the emerging digital era.

This two-day online conference had participation from across the globe including the USA, Australia, Russia, Nigeria, Norwegian, Pakistan, and Bangladesh. The conference received 193 submissions and, following screening, the Technical Program Committee (TPC) received 190 research papers, out of which 44 papers were selected for final presentation after rigorous blind reviews involving more than 240 reviewers. The conference included more than 300 national and international committee chairs, advisory board members, TPC members, keynote speakers, presenters, and experts from across the globe to share their views, innovations, and accomplishments.

We are very grateful to Shri Arif Mohammad Khan, the Governor of Kerala and our Chief Guest on the first day of the conference, and to Shri Ravi Shankar Prasad, the Minister for Communications, Electronics and Information Technology and Law and Justice, Government of India, for sending his kind blessings. We pay our heartfelt gratitude to Vinay Kumar Pathak, Vice Chancellor of the Dr. APJ Abdul Kalam Technical University (formerly UPTU) and our Guest of Honor, Ram Kishore Agarwal and Shri Pankaj Agarwal, our patrons, and our keynote speakers: Rajkumar Buyya, University of Melbourne, Australia, and BalaKrishnan Dasarathy, University of Maryland Global Campus, USA.

We give our special thanks to Shri V. K. Sharma, Arti Noor, and Neha Bajpai from the Center of Development in Advanced Computing (C-DAC), India, for holding the day-long "Special Youth Session" and guiding students on cyber security and its role in handling cyber crime, hardware vulnerabilities and solutions, and cyber safety and privacy protection on social networks.

Our sincere thanks go to all the national and international committee chairs, advisory board members, TPC members, keynote speakers, presenters, and experts from across the globe along with the members of the organizing committee for their cooperation, hard work, and support to make ICCEDE 2020 successful.

We also thank Springer for publishing the proceedings in their Communications in Computer and Information Science (CCIS) series. Last but not least, special thanks to all the authors and participants for their contributions, making an effective, successful, and productive conference.

June 2021

Rajeev Agrawal
Goutam Sanyal
Kevin Curran
Valentina Emilia Balas
Madhu Sharma Gaur

Organization

General Chair

Rajeev Agrawal   G.L Bajaj Institute of Technology and Management, India

Program Chair

Rajkumar Buyya   University of Melbourne, Australia

Conference Secretariat

Sanjeev Kumar   G.L Bajaj Institute of Technology and Management, India

Session Chair for Track 1

Basel Katt   University of Science and Technology, Norway
Vikas Sagar   Chandigarh University, India

Session Chair for Track 2

Emmanuel S. Pilli   Malaviya National Institute of Technology Jaipur, India

Session Chair for Track 3

Ihtiram Raza Khan   Jamia Hamdard University, India
Nishant Kumar   Gurukul Kangri University, India

Session Chair for Track 3

S. K. Pal   DRDO, India
Umang Singh   ITS Ghaziabad, India

Convener

Madhu Sharma Gaur   GL Bajaj Institute of Technology and Management, India

Co-convener

Sanjeev Kumar   GL Bajaj Institute of Technology and Management,
                              India

Internal Advisory Committee

Shashank Awasthi   GL Bajaj Institute of Technology and Management,
                              India
Satyendra Sharma   GL Bajaj Institute of Technology and Management,
                              India
R. K. Mishra   GL Bajaj Institute of Technology and Management,
                              India
P. C. Vashist   GL Bajaj Institute of Technology and Management,
                              India
Sanjeev Pippal   GL Bajaj Institute of Technology and Management,
                              India
Mohit Bansal   GL Bajaj Institute of Technology and Management,
                              India
Vinod Yadav   GL Bajaj Institute of Technology and Management,
                              India
Prashant Mukherjee   GL Bajaj Institute of Technology and Management,
                              India

Internal Screening Committee

Dinesh Kumar Singh   GL Bajaj Institute of Technology and Management,
                              India
Rajiv Kumar   GL Bajaj Institute of Technology and Management,
                              India
Amrita Rai   GL Bajaj Institute of Technology and Management,
                              India
Upendra Dwivedi   GL Bajaj Institute of Technology and Management,
                              India
Paramita De   GL Bajaj Institute of Technology and Management,
                              India
Shivam Mishra   GL Bajaj Institute of Technology and Management,
                              India
Satendra Kumar   GL Bajaj Institute of Technology and Management,
                              India

Organizing Committee

Gaurav Bhaita	GL Bajaj Institute of Technology and Management, India
Sandeep Srivastava	GL Bajaj Institute of Technology and Management, India
Deepak Gupta	GL Bajaj Institute of Technology and Management, India
Lalan Kumar	GL Bajaj Institute of Technology and Management, India
Prem Sagar Sharma	GL Bajaj Institute of Technology and Management, India
Anju Mishra	GL Bajaj Institute of Technology and Management, India
Deepkiran	GL Bajaj Institute of Technology and Management, India
Vikram Singh	GL Bajaj Institute of Technology and Management, India

Technical Program Committee

Aakanksha Sharaff	National Institute of Technology, Raipur, India
Abasiama Godwin Akpan	Evangel University, Nigeria
Abdullahi Arabo	University of the West of England, UK
Abhijit Biswas	Assam University, India
Abhinav Gupta	Jaypee Institute of Information Technology, India
Abhishek Ray	Kalinga Institute of Industrial Technology, India
Ajay Kaul	Shri Mata Vaishno Devi University, India
Akhtar Husain	M.J.P Rohilkahand University, India
Alekha Kumar Mishra	National Institute of Technology, Jamshedpur, India
Amit M. Joshi	Malaviya National Institute of Technology, Jaipur, India
Anand Paul	Kyungpook National Univerist, South Korea
Anandi Giridharan	Indian Institute of Science, India
Angshuman Jana	Indian Institute of Information Technology, Guwahati, India
Anil Kumar Verma	Thapar Institute of Engineering and Technology, India
Anil Singh Parihar	Delhi Technological University, India
Anita Ganpati	Himachal Pradesh University, India
Anita Yadav	Harcourt Butler Technical University, India
Anjan Krishnamurthy	BMS Institute of Technology and Management, India
Anju Yadav	Manipal University Jaipur, India
Anshuman Kalla	Manipal University Jaipur, India
Arka Prakash Mazumdar	Malaviya National Institute of Technology Jaipur, India
Arvind Dhaka	Manipal University Jaipur, India
Ashim Saha	National Institute of Technology, Agartala, India

Ashish Shrivastava	Manipal University Jaipur, India
Avimanyou Vatsa	Fairleigh Dickinson University, USA
B. M. Patil	Maharashtra Institute of Technology, India
B. Surendiran	National Institute of Technology, Pondicherry, India
Badal Soni	National Institute of Technology, Silchar, India
Baijnath Kaushik	Shri Mata Vaishno Devi University, India
Balakrishnan Dasarathy	University of Maryland Global Campus, USA
Balwinder Singh Sodhi	National Institute of Technology, Ropar, India
Basel Katt	Norwegian University of Science and Technology, Norway
Bharat Rawal	Pennsylvania State University, USA
Bhavna Arora	Central University of Jammu, India
Blerim Rexha	University of Prishtina, Kosovo
Brajesh Kumar	M.J.P Rohilkahand University, India
Bruce deGrazia	University of Maryland Global Campus, USA
Chandan Chakraborty	NITTTR, Kolkata, India
Chandrashekhar Azad	National Institute of Technology, Jamshadpur, India
Dac-Nhuong Le	Haiphong University, Vietnam
Dana V. Balas Timar Rad	Aurel Vlaicu University of Arad, Romania
Daya Gupta	Delhi Technological University, India
Deepak Chandra Goel	University of Petroleum and Energy Studies, India
Deepak Singh Tomar	Maulana Azad National Institute of Technology, India
Devesh Katiyar	Dr. Shakuntala Misra National Rehabilitation University, India
Dinesh K. Vishwakarma	Delhi Technological University, India
Dinesh Kumar Tyagi	Malaviya National Institute of Technology Jaipur, India
Divakar Yadav	National Institute of Technology, Hamirpur, India
Dugassa Mulugeta	Addis Ababa University, Ethiopia
Durgesh Mishra	Sri Aurobindo Institute of Technology, India
Faisal Anwer	Aligarh Muslim University, India
Gahangir Hossain	Texas A&M University–Kingsville, USA
Govind P. Gupta	National Institute of Technology, Raipur, India
Gururaj Mukarambi	Central University of Karnataka, India
Harish Ramani	Indian Institute of Information Technology, Bangalore, India
Heechoon Kwon	Korean National Police University, South Korea
Ihtiram Raza Khan	Jamia Hamdard University, India
Imon Mukherjee	Indian Institute of Information Technology, Kalyani, India
Inderjeet Kumar	Graphic Era Hill University, India
J. Amudhavel	VIT University, Bhopal, India
Jitendra V. Tembhurne	Indian Institute of Information Technology, Nagpur, India
Jyoti Grover	Malaviya National Institute of Technology Jaipur, India
K. K. Shukla	Indian Institute of Technology, Varanasi, India
K. Ambujam	Cauvery College of Engineering and Technology, India

Kamal Kumar	National Institute of Technology, Uttarakhand, India
Kamna Solanki	Maharshi Dayanand University, India
Karamjit Bhatia	Gurukula Kangri Vishwavidyalaya, India
Kevin Curran	Ulster University, UK
Kh Johnson Singh	National Institute of Technology, Manipur, India
Kinsuk Giri	NITTTR, Kolkata, India
Kishorjit Nongmeikapam	Indian Institute of Information Technology (IIIT), Manipur, India
Krishan Kumar	National Institute of Technology, Uttarakhand, India
Krishan Kumar Saluja	Panjab University, India
Krishna Pulugurta	Gayatri Vidhya Parishad College of Engineering, India
Kunwar Pal	National Institute of Technology, Sikkim, India
Lata Nautiyal	Suffolk University, UK
M. N. Hoda	BVICAM, India
Madhan Kumar Srinivasan	Accenture, Noida, India
Madhusudan Singh	Yonsei University, South Korea
Mahendra Singh Aswal	Gurukula Kangri Vishwavidyalaya, India
Malaya Dutta Borah	National Institute of Technology, Silchar, India
Maleq Khan	Texas A&M University–Kingsville, USA
Mamoun Alazab	Charles Darwin University, Australia
Mangesh Gonge	Sandeep Institute of Technology and Research Center, India
Manikandan V. M.	Indian Institute of Information Technology, Kottayam, India
Manish Kumar	Punjab Engineering College, India
Manish Sharma	Indian Institute of Technology, Bombay, India
Manju Khari	Netaji Subhas University of Technology, India
Manjula R.	SRM University, India
Manoj Kumar Matho	RCT Institute of Technology, India
Manoj Kumar Singh	DRDO, India
Mansaf Alam	Jamia Millia Islamia, India
Mansur Hasib	University of Maryland Global Campus, USA
Manu Vardhan	National Institute of Technology, Raipur, India
Markus Jakobsson	RavenWhite, USA
Meenakshi Sharma	Chandigarh University, India
Mehdi Soleymani	Arak University, Iran
Minakshi Gogoi	Girijananda Chowdhury Institute of Management and Technology, India
Mohamed Elhoseny	Mansoura University, Egypt
Mohammad S. Alam	Texas A&M University–Kingsville, USA
Mohammad Sajid	Aligarh Muslim University, India
Mohammed Javed	Indian Institute of Information Technology, Allahabad, India
Mohd Sadim	Meerut Institute of Technology, India
Mohit Kumar	National Institute of Technology, Jalandhar, India
Mohit Mittal	Kyoto Sangya University, Japan

Monica Mehrotra	Jamia Millia Islamia, India
Monica R. Mundada	Ramaiah Institute of Technology, India
Mridu Sahu	National Institute of Technology, Raipur, India
Mrinal Kanti Deb Barma	National Institute of Technology, Agartala, India
Murtaza Abbas Rizvi	NITTTR, Bhopal, India
Nagaraju Baydeti	National Institute of Technology, Nagaland, India
Nagarathna A.	National Law School of India University, India
Nagendra Pratap Singh	National Institute of Technology, Hamirpur, India
Namita Tiwari	CSJM University Kanpur, India
Narendra Kohli	Harcourt Butler Technical University, India
Narendra S. Chaudhari	Indian Institute of Technology, Indore, India
Naveen Kumar Gondhi	Shri Mata Vaishno Devi University, India
Neeraj Kumar	Thapar Institute of Engineering and Technology, India
Neeraj Prtap Singh	Merrut Institute of Technology, India
Neeraj Tyagi	Motilal Nehru National Institute of Technology, India
Neetesh Saxena	Georgia Institute of Technology, USA
Nickolas S.	National Institute of Technology, Tiruchirappalli, India
Nikata Singh	Umea University, Sweden
Nilanjan Dey	Techno India College of Technology, India
Nirbhay Chaubey	Gujarat Technological University, India
Nishant Kumar	Gurukul Kangri Vishwavidyalaya, India
P. Venkata Suresh	The Indira Gandhi National Open University, India
P. Krishna Subba Rao	Gayatri Vidya Parishad College of Engineering, India
Panchami V.	Indian Institute of Information Technology, Kottayam, India
Parag Rughani	Gujarat Forensic Sciences University, India
Parkavi A.	M S Ramaiah Institute of Technology, India
Pavan Kumar Mishra	National Institute of Technology, Raipur, India
Phalguni Gupta	Indian Institute of Technology, Kanpur, India
Prabhat Verma	Harcourt Butler Technical University, India
Pradeep Kr Das	Indian Institute of Technology, Guwahati, India
Pradeep Kumar	University of New Brunswick College, Canada
Prahlada Rao B. B.	Rajeev Gandhi Memorial College of Engineering and Technology, India
Pratik Chattopadhyay	Indian Institute of Technology, Varanasi, India
Preeti Malik	Graphic Era Hill University, India
Prerana Mukherjee	Indian Institute of Information Technology, Sri City, India
Prerna Mohit	Indian Institute of Information Technology, Manipur, India
Priyadarshani A. Pattanaik	Telecom SudParis, France
R. Balasubramaniam	Indian Institute of Technology, Roorkee, India
R. C Mittal	JIIT, India
R. C. Joshi	Graphic Era Hill University, India
R. S. Rajput	G.B. Pant University of Agriculture and Technology, India

Rafat Parveen	Jamia Millia Islamia, India
Rafiqual Zaman Khan	Aligarh Muslim University, India
Rajeev Chatterjee	NITTTR, Kolkata, India
Rajendra Hegadi	Indian Institute of Information Technology, Dharwad, India
Rajendra Prasath	Indian Institute of Information Technology, Sri City, India
Rajesh Babu	Gujarat Forensic Sciences University, India
Rajesh N. Phursule	Pimpri Chinchwad College of Engineering, India
Rajitha B.	Motilal Nehru National Institute of Technology, India
Rajkumar Buyya	University of Melbourne, Australia
Rakesh Kumar	Madan Mohan Malaviya University of Technology, India
Raman Singh	Trinity College Dublin, Ireland
Rashid Ali	Aligarh Muslim University, India
Ratneshwer	Jawaharlal Nehru University, India
Ravi Subban	Pondicherry University, India
Ravindra Nath	CSJM University Kanpur, India
Ritesh Agarwal	CSJM University Kanpur, India
Ritesh Bhatia	V4WEB Cybersecurity, India
Rupachandra Singh Thounaojam	Manipur University, India
S. Venkatesan	Indian Institute of Information Technology, Allahabad, India
S. B. Goyal	City University, Malaysia
Saibal Pal	Defence Research and Development Organisation, India
Sajad Khorsandroo	North Carolina A&T State University, USA
Samayveer Singh	National Institute of Technology, Jalandhar, India
Sangram Ray	Indian Institute of Technology, Dhanbad, India
Sanjay Katiyar	Gagotia University, India
Sanjay Sharma	Gautam Buddha University, India
Sanjeev Kumar Prasad	Galgotias University, India
Sansar Singh Chauhan	Galgotias University, India
Sara Paiva	Viana do Castelo Politechnic Institute, Portugal
Saroj Kr. Biswas	National Institute of Technology, Silchar, India
Sartaj Ul Hasan	Indian Institute of Technology, Jammu, India
Sathish Kannan	American University of Sharjah, UAE
Satya Prakash Sahu	National Institute of Technology, Raipur, India
Selena He	Kennesaw State University, USA
Shachi Sharma	South Asian University, India
Shailender Kumar	Delhi Technological University, India
Sharad Saxena	Thapar Institute of Engineering and Technology, India
Shashwati Banerjea	Motilal Nehru National Institute of Technology, India
Shilpa Chaudhari	Ramaiah Institute of Technology, India
Sidney Thompson	Georgetown University, USA

S. K. Hafizul Islam	Indian Institute of Information Technology, Kalyani, India
Somnath Mukhopadhyay	Assam University, India
Sonali Agarwal	Indian Institute of Information Technology, Allahabad, India
Sonali Gupta	YMCA University of Science and Technology, India
Srikant	Sharda University, India
Steffen Wendzel	Hochschule Worms, Germany
Subhasish Dhal	Indian Institute of Information Technology, Guwahati, India
Sunil Vadera	University of Salford, UK
Sunita Sarkar	Assam University, India
Surendra Singh	National Institute of Technology, Uttarakhand, India
Sushil Kumar	Jawaharlal Nehru University, India
Swati Singhal	Gurukula Kangri Vishwavidyalaya, India
Tanupriya	University of Petroleum and Energy Studies, India
Taran Singh Bharti	Jamia Millia Islamia, India
Th. Rupachandra Singh	Manipur University, India
Th. Shanta Kumar	Girijananda Chowdhury Institute of Management and Technology, India
Tirath Prasad Sahu	National Institute of Technology, Raipur, India
Tirthankar Gayen	Jawaharlal Nehru University, India
Tripti Sharma	Inderprastha Engineering College, India
Uche Mbanaso	Nasarawa State University, Nigeria
Uchenna Daniel Ani	University College London, UK
Udai Shanker	Madan Mohan Malaviya University of Technology, India
Umang Singh	Institute of Technology and Science, Ghaziabad, India
Urmila Shrawankar	RTM Nagpur University, India
Uttam Ghosh	Vanderbilt University, USA
V. A. Artamonov	Lomonosov Moscow State University, Russia
V. P. Singh	Thapar Institute of Engineering and Technology, India
V. K. Sharma	C-DAC, India
V. V. Subrahmanyam	The Indira Gandhi National Open University, India
Valentina Emilia Balas	Aurel Vlaicu University of Arad, Romania
Ved Prakash Mishra	Amity University, UAE
Vijay Anant Athavale	Panipat Institute of Engineering and Technology, India
Vijay Bhaskar Semwal	National Institute of Technology, Bhopal, India
Vikas Sagar	Chandigarh University, India
Vinay Kumar	National Institute of Technology, Jamshadpur, India
Vinod Jain	GLA University, India
Virendra Kadyan	University of Petroleum and Energy Studies, India
Vishal Sharma	Singapore University of Technology and Design, Singapore

Vrijendra Singh   Indian Institute of Information Technology, Allahabad,
                                 India
Xiaohua Xu   Kennesaw State University, USA
Yong Shi   Kennesaw State University, USA

Invited Talks

Neoteric Frontiers in Cloud and Edge Computing (Keynote/Plenary)

Rajkumar Buyya

Cloud Computing and Distributed Systems (CLOUDS) Lab,
The University of Melbourne, Australia
Manjrasoft Pvt Ltd, Melbourne, Australia

Abstract. Computing is being transformed to a model consisting of services that are delivered in a manner similar to utilities such as water, electricity, gas, and telephony. In such a model, users access services based on their requirements without regard to where the services are hosted or how they are delivered. Cloud computing paradigm has turned this vision of "computing utilities" into a reality. It offers infrastructure, platform, and software as services, which are made available to consumers as subscription-oriented services. Cloud application platforms need to offer (1) APIs and tools for rapid creation of elastic applications and (2) a runtime system for deployment of applications on geographically distributed computing infrastructure in a seamless manner.

The Internet of Things (IoT) paradigm enables seamless integration of cyber-and-physical worlds and opening up opportunities for creating new class of applications for domains such as smart cities and smart healthcare. The emerging Fog/Edge computing paradigm is extends Cloud computing model to edge resources for latency sensitive IoT applications with a seamless integration of network-wide resources all the way from edge to the Cloud.

This keynote presentation will cover (a) 21st century vision of computing and identifies various IT paradigms promising to deliver the vision of computing utilities; (b) innovative architecture for creating elastic Clouds integrating edge resources and managed Clouds, (c) Aneka 5G, a Cloud Application Platform, for rapid development of Cloud/Big Data applications and their deployment on private/public Clouds with resource provisioning driven by SLAs, (d) a novel FogBus software framework with Blockchain-based data-integrity management for facilitating end-to-end IoT-Fog/Edge-Cloud integration for execution of sensitive IoT applications, (e) experimental results on deploying Cloud and Big Data/ IoT applications in engineering, and health care (e.g., COVID-19), deep learning/Artificial intelligence (AI), satellite image processing, natural language processing (mining COVID-19 research literature for new insights) and smart cities on elastic Clouds; and (f) directions for delivering our 21st century vision along with pathways for future research in Cloud and Edge/Fog computing.

Speaker Biography and Photo

 is a Redmond Barry Distinguished Professor and Director of the Cloud Computing and Distributed Systems (CLOUDS) Laboratory at the University of Melbourne, Australia. He is also serving as the founding CEO of Manjrasoft, a spin-off company of the University, commercializing its innovations in Cloud Computing. He has authored over 750 publications and seven text books including "Mastering Cloud Computing" published by McGraw Hill, China Machine Press, and Morgan Kaufmann for Indian, Chinese and international markets respectively. Dr. Buyya is one of the highly cited authors in computer science and software engineering worldwide (h-index = 147, g-index = 322, **113,600+** citations). "A Scientometric Analysis of Cloud Computing Literature" by German scientists ranked Dr. Buyya as the World's Top-Cited (#1) Author and the World's Most-Productive (#1) Author in Cloud Computing. Dr. Buyya is recognised as Web of Science "Highly Cited Researcher" for four consecutive years since 2016, IEEE Fellow, Scopus Researcher of the Year 2017 with Excellence in Innovative Research Award by Elsevier, and the "Best of the World", in Computing Systems field, by The Australian 2019 Research Review.

Software technologies for Grid, Cloud, and Fog computing developed under Dr. Buyya's leadership have gained rapid acceptance and are in use at several academic institutions and commercial enterprises in 50 countries around the world. Dr. Buyya has led the establishment and development of key community activities, including serving as foundation Chair of the IEEE Technical Committee on Scalable Computing and five IEEE/ACM conferences. These contributions and international research leadership of Dr. Buyya are recognized through the award of "2009 IEEE Medal for Excellence in Scalable Computing" from the IEEE Computer Society TCSC. Manjrasoft's Aneka Cloud technology developed under his leadership has received "Frost & Sullivan New Product Innovation Award". He served as founding Editor-in-Chief of the IEEE Transactions on Cloud Computing. He is currently serving as

Editor-in-Chief of Software: Practice and Experience, a long standing journal in the field established ~50 years ago. For further information on Dr. Buyya, please visit his cyberhome: www.buyya.com.

A Comparative Study of Machine Learning Techniques in Cyberthreat and Cyberattack Detection

Balakrishnan Dasarathy

University of Maryland Global Campus, Adelphi, MD 08854, USA
balakrishnan.dasarathy@faculty.umgc.edu

Abstract. This talk is on applying leading machine learning (ML) techniques to detect cyberthreats and cyberattacks. The talk begins with a short overview of three leading supervisory techniques, Logistic Regression, Neural Network (NN) and Support Vector Machine, and one unsupervised learning technique, the Multivariate Gaussian Distribution, that are applied. NSL-KDD datasets used for training, validation and testing are then described. Potential alternatives to these commonly used datasets for benchmarking ML algorithms for cyber-security are also discussed. Metrics used to assess the algorithms, precision, recall and accuracy, are then defined. An overview of bias vs. variance tradeoff to get optimal results with the algorithms is then provided. The performance of the ML algorithms applied is then described. The performance of the NN algorithm for two-class classification (normal vs. attack) and the anomaly detection using the Multivariate Gaussian Distribution function is encouraging. A main goal of the future research is to improve performance in classifying attacks into their constituent classes, i.e., to develop more accurate signatures or models for attack classes. The future work will also include applying the algorithms to CIC-IDS2017, a recent dataset with data on several attacks that are common today.

Keywords: Cyber-attacks and threats · Machine learning · Intrusion detection · Applying machine learning for threat and attack detection

Bio: Professor Balakrishnan Dasarathy has been with the University of Maryland Global Campus (UMGC) since September 2012. He has managed and directed a graduate school program in Cybersecurity at UMGC. Prior to joining UMGC, he has had more than thirty years of industry R&D and R&D Management experience in in the telecom (GTE Labs, Bellcore and Telcordia) and finance (JP Morgan) industries. He has applied his cybersecurity, software and network engineering and machine learning skills to commercial and military systems. Dr. Dasarathy's PhD is in Computer and Information Science from the Ohio State University. His LinkedIn Profile is at: http://www.linkedin.com/in/bdasarathyprofile.

Cyber Ranges and Security Testbeds

Basel Katt

Department of Information Security and Comm. Tech.
Norwegian University of Science and Technology (NTNU), Norway

Abstract. Digitization has been one of the main issues we have been facing recently, especially, in the COVID19 era and beyond. With the increased usage of ICT infrastructure in the digitized society, cyber security attacks and threats are increasing and becoming more sophisticated, advanced and server. To deal with this new threat landscape, there is an urgent need for increasing cyber security education and training, and including the whole society in cyber security awareness programs. To facilitate the increased demand on cyber security training, education, and awareness, cyber ranges can be used. A cyber range is an arena where cyber security training, exercise, testing and research can be conducted. In particular, it facilitates and enables the execution of cyber security exercises, labs and competitions by supporting planning and execution activities and automating the scenario infrastructure creation. The aim of this talk to introduce the concept of cyber ranges and their main goals and usages with the results of a systematic literature review aiming at looking at cyber range architectures, tools, scenarios, and functions. The presentation will first discuss the security skill shortage that we face in our society and industry these days. Then, it will discuss potential strategies to deal with and tackle this shortage, proposing cyber ranges as a major tool and facilitator in this area. Then, cyber security exercise lifecycle will be discussed, and the cyber range taxonomy will be presented and elaborated. The taxonomy will include 6 main areas of focus, or perspectives, which are: (1) scenario, (2) environment, (3) management, (4) teaming, (5) learning, and (6) monitoring. I would conclude with emphasizing on the importance of cyber security training in our society and the importance of tools and systems like cyber ranges in this area.

Contents

Cyber Security Issues and Challenges in Emerging Digital Era

Empirical Findings of Assessment of Critical Infrastructure Degree of Dependency on ICT

Uche Magnus Mbanaso [iD] and Victor Emmanuel Kulugh[(✉)] [iD]

Centre for Cyberspace Studies, Nasarawa State University, Keffi, Nigeria
uche.magnus@mbanaso.org, kulughvictore@nsuk.edu.ng

Abstract. This paper presents an assessment of the degree of dependency of Critical Infrastructure (CI) on Information and Communications Technology (ICT). The assessment used the ICT Dependency Model, and a software tool based on the model to measure the degree of ICT dependency grounded on predefined metrics and indicators. The outcomes are the ICT Dependency Index (IDI) - a composite value of the quantitative summation of the metrics, the ICT Dependency Quadrant (IDQ) - a mechanism that comparatively groups the IDI into four bands represented as quadrants i.e. Q1, Q2, Q3, and Q4, which depicts the intersection of dependency and cyber risk. The Q4 quad demonstrates a high degree of ICT dependency, and consequently a potential high cyber risk. Q1 depicts low ICT dependency with a corresponding potential low cyber risk. The results show that increasing level of ICT dependency by CIs has the potential to exacerbate their cyber risk as depicted by the 20 organisations in Q3 and Q4 quad-bands. Consequently, the quantitative approach helps to comparatively assess, group, and visualize the degree of dependency of CI sectors and organisations in a more intuitive fashion using the IDI and IDQ. The IDI and IDQ establish the threshold of ICT dependency and potential cyber risk in a single view. Our solution applies scientific and empirical tools for continuously measuring and ranking ICT dependency of sectors and their organisations in a universal and repeatable fashion. This process can eliminate bias and facilitate proportionate national investment in critical information infrastructure protection (CIIP).

Keywords: Nigeria · Critical sector · Critical infrastructure · Critical information infrastructure · ICT dependency

1 Introduction

Uninterrupted operation of Critical Infrastructure (CI) is a cardinal economic and security objective of every nation-state. The failure, disruption or degradation of a single CI can have monumental negative consequences on national security, economy and wellbeing of citizens [1–3]. However, according to [4], the growing dependence on information and communications technology (ICT) has influenced the increasing interconnectedness of modern CIs and integrations; thus, exacerbating the threat landscape with intriguing cyber risks occasioned by the inherent ICT vulnerabilities. It is that those disruptive cyber events are characterised by some elements of surprise and urgency with high risks

© Springer Nature Switzerland AG 2021
R. Agrawal et al. (Eds.): ICCEDE 2020, CCIS 1436, pp. 3–23, 2021.
https://doi.org/10.1007/978-3-030-84842-2_1

[5]. Consequently, modern CIs dependency on ICT requires proportionate protections against unforeseen cyber events capable of causing damages of high magnitude. Thus, the provision of the necessary protection, requires that the extent of CIs' dependency on ICT using a scientific and empirical measurement to ascertain the importance of ICT to organisations is vital. The continuous evaluation of the increasing degree of dependency of CIs such as electricity, water, transportation, education, financial services, intelligence, security, etc. on ICT [6], is essential to Critical Information Infrastructure Protection (CIIP).

Emerging technologies like the Internet of Things (IoT), Smart Grids, Industrial Control Systems (ICS), Cloud Computing, 5G and Smart Cities will further exacerbate CI cyber risks as they will potentially amplify CI dependency on ICT. Consequently, the unavailability, disruption or destruction of ICT- enabled systems even for the shortest period has the potentials for catastrophic failures of huge proportion, which may result to cascading and escalating effects [7, 8]. In [9], it is argued that critical sectors are sturdily dependent on ICT infrastructure by evolution and opportunism without foresight and adequate planning. As a result, the security and safety of the ICT systems are not usually envisioned *ab initio*. However, a key requirement for CIIP should be to understand the extent of the inherent vulnerability of ICT systems [10, 11] due to dependency. So, the expectation is that CI should have the ability to maintain a reasonable acceptable level of operation in the face of disruptions including deliberate cyberattacks, operational overload, misconfiguration, and equipment failures [11, 12]. Thus, for CI-ICT interconnected to support a modern society, it requires the guaranteed operational correctness within the interlace of the underlying ICT systems.

In Nigeria, despite the increasing digitalisation of traditional operations and emergence of critical information infrastructure (CII), empirical study in this area is overly limited. Research-based information regarding CII is unavailable in the public domain. More so, there is no publicly available empirical evidence of growing CI dependency on ICT, in a manner that critical sector managers can scientifically gauge the level of organisational ICT dependence. The implication is that any protection strategy that is not empirically supported can result in a false sense of security. Critical sector organisations need to continuously estimate the level of ICT dependency to further appreciate the potential cyber risks they may face. To fill this void, this article presents ICT quantitative dependency assessment leveraging a Dependency tool developed by our research team [13]. Three metrics are implemented i.e. *Adoption, Integration* and *Automation* to reflect various maturity of ICT provision. Each metric has indicators as units of quantifiable measurements. The survey inputs from the critical sector organisations formed the basis for the computation of various organisational ICT Dependency Index (IDI) based on the mathematical constructs of the model.

The various organisational IDI scores are comparatively grouped using our ICT Dependency Quadrant (IDQ) scheme. The IDQ shows the grouped IDI scores of organisations in a single view. The exceptionality of this approach is that the methodology is adaptable, scientific and empirical, which depicts the properties of repeatability and transparency. The repeatability quality guarantees that all sectors and organisation are measured based on the same metrics and indicators, thereby ensuring reliability. More so, the results of successive assessments of sectors or organisations using the same parameter settings and measurement should lie within unobjectionable variations. This provides the avenue for a comparative single view of different ICT dependency levels of diverse sectors and organisations. The advantage is that a country can relatively ascertain the various ICT dependency status of critical sector organisations in support of national effort towards effective CIIP.

The rest of the paper is organised as follows: Sect. 2 provides background and related works to the study; Sect. 3 describes the methodological approach, and Sect. 4 is the description of the computational model, Sect. 5 presents the results. Section 6, presents findings, analyses and discussions; Sect. 7 concludes the paper.

2 Background and Related Works

Globally, critical infrastructures face increased risk [2, 14]. A combination of factors account for the increasing CI-related risk; namely: urbanisation which stresses the utilisation of old infrastructures to their limits; the increasing interwovenness and dependencies of infrastructural services; the desire of the population to have services available anytime, anywhere [15]. Thus, meeting the above goals requires an increased utilisation of ICT to improve efficiency, productivity, and accessibility; support for new services and general optimization of the capacity of the CIs [13, 15] and to support, monitor, control and increase CI functionalities [16]. The upshot of this is increased interconnectedness of CIs through ICT. Consequently, it introduces new dimensions of dependencies and interdependencies amongst CIs and ICT [17]. Similarly, it has expanded the dependency and interdependency of CIs in chains [18, 19]. According to [9], this has created the cyber organisational layer for CIs in a way that the cyber layer is becoming one of the most important sources of interdependencies amidst other organisational layers. Traditionally, the cyber elements are inherently vulnerable to malicious exploitation [20], making cyberattacks a major threat to CI systems with potentials for cascading failures [9]. Consequently, the risk of even a minor disruption in a single CI can lead to catastrophic cascading or escalating failures of CI networks [21]. The speed at which ICT systems process data further exacerbate the potential consequences arising from cyberattacks on CIs coupled with the fact that cyberattacks, unlike physical attacks can go unnoticed over time, further amplifying the risk of heavy dependency on cyber systems [22].

Over the years, cyber threat actors have taken undue advantage of the inherent cyber vulnerabilities to degrade, abuse or destroy the CIs to the detriment of the owners, operators and the population [23, 24]. For instance, a rogue nation can leverage vulnerabilities in cyber systems to undermine the security of the CIs of rival or enemy nations [25]. Invariably, attacks such as advanced persistent attacks (APTs) on CIs may go over a long period undetected [26, 27]. Additionally, terrorist organisations do take unjustified advantage of cyber weaknesses to carry out nefarious activities against states [28]. Similarly, cybercriminal groups can equally exploit a weakness in ICT systems to gain undesired benefits [29]. Emerging technologies such as the IoT, promising to exponentially increase the integration and interconnectedness of physical infrastructures will exacerbate security concerns in CIs. And with 5G technology [9, 30], security may worsen exponentially. According to [9], these are bringing fresh risks as the cybersecurity maturity of emerging technologies remains very low. In most cases, security is not thoroughly considered at the initial design and implementations by default. The share expansion of the cyberattack surface created by emerging cyber-physical systems has heightened the risk landscape.

The Ukrainian power grid attack in December 2015 is an example of the cyberattack on CI that had cascading consequences, leading to a total power blackout and impacted other CIs and the population [31]. Often, the financial sector cyberinfrastructure across the globe have suffered unprecedented cyberattacks exploiting inherent flaws in cyber systems [32]. Also, the electricity power blackouts in North America, and Canada in 2003, was due to cyberattacks that disrupted the ICT system and failed to provide real-time diagnostic support [33]. The failure cascaded into several geographical regions as well as impacted the operation of other CIs significantly.

There are ongoing research efforts to understand and address cyber risks as a result of growing CI dependency on ICT. Although there is a rising consensus within the CI research community that the increasing interdependencies of CIs are fuelled by continuous integration of emerging ICT systems [2, 34, 35] is bringing huge complexity. However, most research efforts have concentrated on qualitative assessment, which limits the quantification of CIs dependency on ICT. Also, other research efforts geared towards usage measurement of ICT by populations such as the network readiness index (NRI) [36], which assesses the preparedness of nations, and how they continuously leverage emerging technologies to reap the benefits presented by digital revolution and evolution [37]. Similarly, the Global Cybersecurity Index (GCI) measures the cybersecurity readiness of member countries [38].

Although the work of [32] proposed a framework that identifies dependencies of an organization on technological infrastructures, for evaluating the business impact of any possible failure, the work did not employ any scientific metrics for the evaluation. Similar work by [39] also studied Critical Dependencies of Energy, Finance and Transport Infrastructure on ICT Infrastructure but was not based on any computational model, and was not supported by empirical data to quantify the CI level of dependency on ICT. Thus, the paper describes a computational model to assess the CI degree of dependency on ICT quantitatively. The quantification of the extent of a CI's dependency on ICT, and in comparison, with other CIs is vital to nationally prioritise CIIP since not all CIs will have the same characteristics and equal criticality. The quantitative assessment of CI dependency on ICT is an integral part of our ongoing study on CNI and Cybersecurity. The bottom-goal is to provide a scientific and empirical approach in the comparative quantification of CIs dependency on ICT that is universal and repeatable geared towards national comprehensive CIIP (Table 1).

3   Research Methodology

The assessment is based on computational ICT Dependency tool [13] based on three metrics i.e. *Adoption*, *Integration* and *Automation*. The constructs of the model provide mathematical elements that form the development of data structures, algorithms and the software tool. An instrument designed based on the three metrics and indicators- the unit of measure based on a ratio scale provided the data generation mechanism. The

Table 1. Summary of related works

#	Citation	Focus	Gap
1	[2]	The authors argue that there is an increased level of ICT adoption in CI and that this has the potential to exacerbate the risk profile of CI	The work did not proffer solution on how this dependency can be evaluated towards measuring the potential risk associated with ICT dependency
2	[33]	This paper contends that ICT infrastructure underpinning CIs are increasing the complexity of vulnerability and threats	The authors failed to provide a concrete approach on how to evaluate the level of dependence of CIs on ICT amidst the vulnerability and threat landscapes
3	[34]	This article agrees that CIs are increasingly getting interconnected through technology and this potentially portends risk for the connected CIs	The work falls short of proposing ways to measure the level of connectivity and the associated risk
4	[35]	The authors presented the usage measurement of ICT by populations	This measurement based on qualitative method did not attempt to highlight the potential cyber risk the population may face in the usage of ICT
5	[36]	The authors assessed the preparedness of nations, and how they continuously leverage emerging technologies to reap the benefits presented by the digital revolution and evolution	The paper highlighted the preparedness of nations without any attempt to measure the relative level of the preparedness and the potential risk associated with the digital revolution
6	[37]	This paper discusses the assessment of the cybersecurity preparedness of nations	The paper failed to propose a way to measure the dependency of CIs on ICT
7	[31]	The authors propose a framework that identifies the dependencies of an organisation on technological infrastructures as the basis for evaluating the business impact of any possible failure	The paper never mentioned any scientific tool for the quantification of the degree of organisational dependency on ICT, and the potential impact the failures can cause the organisation
8	[38]	This paper presented a study on Critical Dependencies of Energy, Finance and Transport on ICT infrastructure	The article focused on the conceptualisation of dependencies with less emphasis on the scientific model or tool that can quantify the degree of ICT dependency

questionnaire, which was divided into thematic areas based on the metrics, and the indicators represented the input selection parameters to the quantitative software tool. Consequently, the questionnaire, which is embedded in the software tool was administered to 27 organisations from 9 sectors with at least 3 participants from each organisation. The rationale to use a minimum of 3 participants from each organisation during the data collection is to minimize bias that may arise from the use of a single participant per organisation. For computing organisational ICT Dependency Index (IDI), the resulting scores from the participants per organisation are averaged to form IDI of that organisation. The tool allows for real-time data collection and processing, which automatically computes and analyse the Dependency Factor (DF) scores of the metrics, and subsequently compute the IDI scores. This is followed by the classification and grouping of IDI into the constituent quadrants. Additionally, the real-time computation places the sectors and organisations to their respective quads based on the IDI scores.

4   The Computational Model

In Fig. 1, the ICT Dependency model showing various components, and how they interrelate is presented. There are four principal components, each comprising sub-components designed to provide more in-depth measurements. The dependency assessment metrics define the thematic areas of measurement, the computation component calculates the values derived from the metrics, the variable items of measure reflect the various indicators. The descriptions of the components are as follows:

4.1   Critical Infrastructure Characterisation

The characterisation of critical infrastructure is an important step towards correct identification of key functions or services the infrastructure provides [39]. In some cases, the required information may be obtained from publicly available sources. The characterisation helps to situate the core mission of the organisation or an asset, which potentially indicate the commitment of an organisation in terms of her digital transformation [40]. The ICT Dependency characterisation followed a two-step approach:

i.   Identification, analysis and characterisation of tangible assets, vital services or functions that depend on ICT with emphasis on physical infrastructure;
ii. ICT-dependency assessment based on three metrics – *Adoption, Integration* and *Automation,* which provide in-depth quantification of variable attributes of measurement in more granularity.

4.2   Dependency Assessment Metric

This is a construct that measures dependency factors at various phases of ICT provisioning. Each metric has sub-elements followed by indicators; an indicator is a concrete granular attribute that is measurable, called the *Dependency Indicator (DI).* Similarly, a metric is simply an abstract contributory measurable factor, somewhat, a pillar that aggregates sub-elements and diverse indicators [41]. The outcome referred to as *Dependency Factor (DF)* is the summation of the sub-elements and their indicators. The following section describes the pillars of the dependency assessment metrics (DAM).

I.   **Adoption**: The term adoption is used here to connote the corporate mission of an organisation to leverage ICT for operational efficiency and high productivity

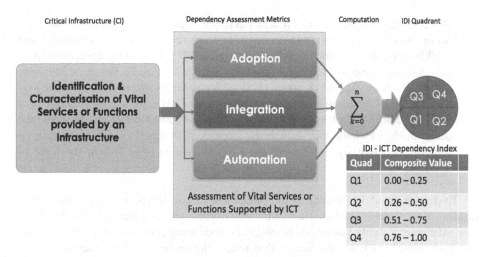

Fig. 1. ICT Dependency model

[42]. Due to the complexity of ICT provisioning, planning for digital transformations should be considered methodically, such as adapting Technology Acceptance Model (TAM), which can be the basis to conceptualise the anticipated utility of the technology [15]. Thus, an organisation needs to articulate the business value such transformation will bring to bear on the mission and core objectives of the organisation [43]. Consequently, the *Adoption* metric incorporates the indicators that quantify the variable parameters that define the acceptance and implementation of digital transformation. To this extent, the study considered elements such as ICT roadmap, ICT policy, ICT Security policy, awareness, training, and foundational ICT infrastructural components [20].

II. **Integration**: ICT integration refers to the degree or extent to which ICT has been embedded into an organization's processes and operations [44]. The level of integration is determined by the interplay between users and the technology infrastructure across the enterprise ecosystem. *Integration* can be measured in an organisational context by the availability of basic ICT systems, accessibility and the personnel skill set that can help achieve organisational objectives. It implies that at the organisational level, *Integration* can be measured based on the overall operational use of ICT for greater efficiency and productivity [15]. Such parameters that can be considered include the availability of network (LAN) concerning the number of devices or nodes connected to the LAN, access to public network [45], web presence, availability of assets and identity management systems. The thrust is that integrating the core operations of an organisation, its services and functions increases the cyber risks exposure of the organisation.

III. **Automation**: Today the ubiquitous influence of the Internet has brought about the notion of fourth utility revolution, making the Internet, the most indispensable technology of the modern society. It implies that core services and functions require unified integration, which both people and physical objects are increasingly being interconnected to enhance efficiency and productivity. Consequently,

ICT automation is becoming a functional requirement for most organisations [46]. *Automation* in this context is a measure of how an organisation improve operational workflow to reduce human interventions by pre-setting many of the operational processes to self-drive. In [15], such functions include *Enterprise Resource Planning (ERP), Decision Support Systems (DSS), Electronic Inventory Management Systems (EIMS), Participatory Project Management (PPM), Knowledge Management Systems (KMS),* which automate the workflow of most operations. Besides, the use of modern technologies such as the Internet of Things (IoT), Radio Frequency Identification (RFID) and Near Field Communication (NFC), help the level of automation.

To deepen the understanding of the model and its constructs, we conceptualise the framing of the variable attributes in an attempt to formalise the mathematical and computational elements. Table 2 describes briefly, the Dependency Assessment Metrics (DAM) and each contributory weight factors that reflect the influence of the metrics in ICT dependency quantification.

Table 2. Descriptions of dependency assessment metrics

#	Dependency Metrics	Abbreviation	Description	Weights (%)	Weight factor (w_f)
1	Adoption	*Ade*	This depicts the organisation's readiness to adopt ICT as a viable operational tool for improved productivity and efficiency but little or none has been implemented	25	0.25
2	Integration	*Ine*	This portrays that integration of ICT functions and features into the core operations of a particular organisation has been considerably achieved and equally with high potential cyber risks	35	0.35
3	Automation	*Aue*	This indicates the full integration and automation of core business operations using ICT functions and features and potentially is inclined to very high cyber risks	40	0.40
	Total			**100**	**1.00**

The criteria for the arbitrary assignments of weights is based on the fact that the effect of cyber risk is unlikely to have the same impact on the metrics. Seemingly, from a cyber-security risk perspective, and the degree of ICT dependency, the impact of failure cannot be distributed equally across the metrics. This assumption strengthens the argument that an organisation with a high level of *Automation* is likely to be more susceptible to cyber threat than an organisation with a high level of *Integration* but low level of *Automation*. A similar argument holds for *Adoption* in comparison to *Integration*; implying that an organisation with a high level of *Integration*, is likely to have a higher cyber risk than an organisation with a high level of *Adoption* but low level of *Integration*. Thus, we can argue that there is a correlation between the degree of dependency and the cyber risk (impact of failure concerning contributory factors of the metrics). Consequently, the potentiality of cyber risk factors influenced the weighting factors of the metrics, which is a measure of the impact of failures invariance of the metric causative factors.

Dependency Indicator (DI). The DI is the unit of measure based on a quantitative five-range ratio scale. It captures in quantitative terms the effect of exact dependency attributes, depicting the level of achievement of that particular indicator in context. This concept is adapted from [45], the guidance for performance measurement of information security metrics, of which the goal is the cogency of the quantification. Consequently, this provides a uniform repeatable process, which contextuality extends the organisational view of ICT dependency. The quantitative scale in consideration of DI is shown in Table 3.

Table 3. Dependency Indicator (DI) scale

Qualitative	Quantitative	Description
None	0	None existence – complete absence, implying quantitatively a zero attribute of measure
Low	2	Has little attribute value of measure to the organisational operation, function or service
Moderate	3	The modest attribute value of measure to the organisational operation, function or service
High	4	Indication of the substantive attribute value of measure to the organisational operation, function or service
Very High	5	Implies a mission-critical attribute value of measure to the organisational operation, function or service

4.3 Computation Model

The computation model calculates the ICT Dependency Index (IDI) based on the summation of assessment metrics and indicators. The underlying mathematical constructs described in Sect. 4 shows the stepwise mathematical formulae for the various stages of computation to arrive at the IDI. The IDI provides a composite value of the degree of an organisational dependence on ICT. The selection of the *DI* follows a ratio scale of 0 – 5, where 0 implies the none existence or absences of an indicator, and 5 is the possible highest value of a measure. The IDI provides the basis for the comparative analysis of the quantification of ICT dependency of sectors and organisations. Again, interpreting the *DI* scale in terms of cybersecurity risks, implies that 0 value connotes zero dependencies and zero risks, while 5 connotes potentially high risk and high dependency.

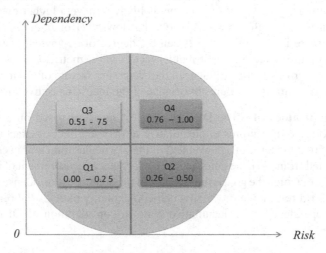

Fig. 2. ICT Dependency Quadrant (IDQ)

4.4   The ICT Dependency Quadrant (IDQ)

The IDQ concept is shown in Fig. 2, which offers the mechanism for a single view of IDIs of various organisations. The concept of the quadrant is to provide a four-band scale based on proportional dependency and risk. It simplifies a way to rank and benchmark various organisation's ICT dependency in a comparative and repeatable manner. In this way, the IDI of organisations from different sectors can be compared in a risk-view manner. That is, the IDQ exposes the ICT dependency of an organisation concerning other organisations, even though the organisations may unlikely belong to the same sector. More so, the IDQ can offer the advantage of comparative analysis of sectors and organisations in a single assessment. The full explanation of the quads is provided in Table 4.

The IDQ depicts that ICT dependency can be directly proportional to cyber risk, i.e., the higher the dependency, the higher the potential cyber risk. Thus, organisations that fall under Q1 are less dependent on ICT, which implies that cyber risk is low. In contrast, Q4 depicts an organisation with a high degree of ICT dependency, with a concomitant potential high cyber risk. The novelty of IDQ draws from the fact that it is a comparative risk-view tool that can help a country to be more proactive in its cybersecurity plan by providing incentives for high-risk organisations. Again, infrastructure may be vital but

Table 4. ICT Dependency Quadrant (IDQ) description

Quadrant	Composite Values	Note
Q1	0.00 – 0.25	The organisation is in a very low use of ICT features and functions. This quad connotes lower ICT dependency and cyber risks
Q2	0.26 – 0.50	This demonstrates low use of ICT features and functions and without consistent and structural ICT management. Considerably, important elements of ICT are missing. This quad implies high risk with low ICT dependency
Q3	0.51 – 0.75	The ICT features and functions are structurally implemented and integrated into the core organisation's operations but with fewer elements missing. This quad depicts high use of ICT implying high ICT dependency and cyber risks
Q4	0.76 – 1.00	Critical operations, services and functions are ICT-enabled and automated. This quad implies very high ICT dependency and cyber risks

may have potentially low cybersecurity exposure. Thus, prioritisation can be given to highly ICT-dependent entities in terms of resources for proportionate protection.

4.5 The ICT Dependency Mathematical Model

This section provides formally, the taxonomy of ICT-dependency quantitative measurement, with mathematical and standardised parameters. This aims to provide a scientific but repeatable and transparent measurement mechanism influenced by common criteria. This provides the basis to calculate the bands of ICT-dependency based on a scale of degree of preference since all CIs cannot have equal degree of ICT dependency.

Formal Definitions. The following variables are defined to help formulate the mathematical equations:

I. *Dependency Indicator (DI)*: DI is the quantitative evaluation of the degree of dependency of a particular indicator, in the scale of $0 - 5$, which is the granular unit of measure;
II. *Dependency Factor (DF)*: DF is the summation of the various DIs - the indicators of a particular Dependency Metric (DM). The DF is usually normalised to give a composite value which lies between 0.00 and 1.00.;
III. *ICT Dependency Index (IDI):* This is the weighted summation of the DMs (or the main pillars)- the computational summation based on DFs and weighted factors assigned to the DMs. The scores of IDI lies between 0.00 and 1.00.

Mathematical Equations

Dependency Factor (DF)

The *DF* is the summation of the *DIs* of a particular Dependency Metric (DM) and can be represented mathematically as shown in Eq. 1.

$$DF = \sum_{i=1}^{n} DI_i \tag{1}$$

Where i = 1 to n, and n is the number of DIs being measured

To normalise *DF* to a composite value, Eq. 1 can be modified such that:

$$DF_0 = \frac{DF}{z} \tag{2}$$

scale ratio Q. As shown in Table 2, Q is 5, it follows that Z can be derived thus:

$$Z = 5N \tag{3}$$

Therefore, substituting Z in Eq. (2), DF_0 thus becomes:

$$DF_0 = \frac{DF}{5N} \tag{4}$$

Where N is the number of indicators of a particular metric being measured, and N can be said to be a derivable variable constant.

The ICT Dependency Index (IDI)

The *IDI* is the sum of the *DFs*, which is the summation of the contributing effects of the *DFs*. Thus:

$$IDI = w_i \sum_{i=1}^{n} DF_0 i \tag{5}$$

Where i = 1 to n and n is the number of DFs, in this c(ase n = 3 i.e. adoption (Ade), integration (Ine) and automation (Aue), and $w_i$is the weight factor of each metrics as shown in Table 2. Therefore, Eq. (3)becomes:

$$IDI = [(DF0Ade)(wAde)] + [(DF0Ine)(wIne)] + [(DF0Aue)(wAue)] \tag{6}$$

The weights factors of the DMs are assigned as stated in Table 2, the w_i can be substituted in Eq. (4) as follows:

$$IDI = 0.25(DF0Ade) + 0.35(DF0Ine) + 0.40(DF0Aue) \tag{7}$$

Thus, *IDI* lies between $(0.00 \le IDI \le 1.00)$, which represents the composite ICT Dependency Index (IDI) value of a particular organisation.

5   Data Presentation

Table 5 shows a summary of organisations that participated in the survey. Also, Table 5 shows that out of the 50 organisations invited for the survey, 27 participated. Table 6 shows the result of the survey, depicting the IDI scores of organisations and their placement in the quadrant (IDQ). Notably, the organisations have been masked with codes for confidentiality and privacy considerations. Table 6, reveals that IDI scores of 3 organisations are above 0.75, which place them in Q4 quad. Similarly, the IDI scores of 20 organisations lie between 0.51 and 0.75 to fall in Q3 quad, which represents 74.07% of organisations surveyed. Likewise, 3 organisations scored between 0.26 and 0.50 while 1 organisation scored below 0.26, thus falling in Q2 and Q1 quads respectively as depicted in Fig. 3. It can be noted that the scores depicting ICT dependency cut across the 9 categories (or sectors), implying that ICT dependency can as well be visualised and viewed on a sector basis.

Table 5. Summary of CI organisations and respondents

#	Category	No. of Organisations	Respondents
'1	MDAs	25	11
2	States	2	1
3	Communications/Media	2	1
4	ICT/Telecoms	3	2
5	Security and Safety	5	2
6	Education	3	4
7	Health	2	1
8	Electricity	7	4
9	Axillary	1	1
	Total	**50**	**27**

In Table 7, the individual scores of ICT dependency assessments metrics used in the survey i.e. *Adoption, Integration* and *Automation*, which form the basis for data collection for the measurement of CI dependency on ICT is shown. The composite value of the IDI presented in Table 6 is the summation of the computed ICT dependency metrics (or Dependency Factors (DF) based on equation 6 and 7 respectively. The chart in Fig. 4 shows the organisations' IDI values and their respective quads. The trend shows that majority of organisations fall into Q3. The next section 6 throws more insight into the results and the findings.

6   Findings, Analysis and Discussions

Figure 4 shows organisations according to respective ICT Dependency Index (IDI) scores based on Table 6, which illustrates the distribution of large concentration of organisations

Table 6. Survey dataset showing organisations, sectors, IDI scores and quadrants

#	Organisation Code	Category	IDI Score	Quadrants
1	VRJKP	Communications & Media	0.88	Q4
2	DUOHX	MDA	0.79	Q4
3	ULOWF	MDA	0.78	Q4
4	XNBPM	MDA	0.75	Q3
5	ZLPSV	MDA	0.75	Q3
6	UVEWC	Information Technology	0.73	Q3
7	ULMJG	MDA	0.73	Q3
8	THZDG	Security & Safety	0.73	Q3
9	AXKUN	MDA	0.72	Q3
10	PPJIW	MDA	0.71	Q3
11	NGDYE	Energy	0.70	Q3
12	ZREMB	Education	0.66	Q3
13	CROEX	Education	0.66	Q3
14	DDVPK	MDA	0.66	Q3
15	KCCEM	Energy	0.65	Q3
16	SVGVC	MDA	0.63	Q3
17	AGPXU	Education	0.61	Q3
18	FXBQV	Education	0.59	Q3
19	FXFMY	Energy	0.58	Q3
20	JXZNL	Health	0.58	Q3
21	GYNNY	Auxiliary Sectors	0.56	Q3
22	WVLGY	State	0.54	Q3
23	XQLAR	Security & Safety	0.53	Q3
24	NCHHK	MDA	0.47	Q2
25	FKVQH	Energy	0.47	Q2
26	LFKRM	MDA	0.33	Q2
27	VVZEN	MDA	0.08	Q1

(20 precisely) in Q3 and only 3 organisations in Q4 quad. The Q3 quad-band implies a high degree of ICT dependency and a corresponding potential high cyber risk. While the 3 organisations in Q4 depict very high use of ICT with core functions and services that are integrated and automated imply potential very high cyber risks, organisations Q1 quad-band represents low ICT usage, and subsequently, potentially low cyber risks. This way, the result is insightful in the sense that a particular IDQ (or quad) can cut

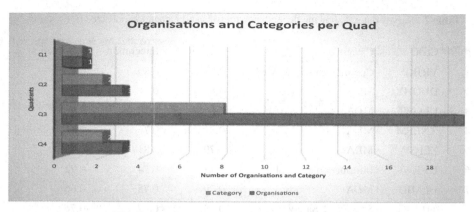

Fig. 3. Number sectors and organisations per quad

across sectors as exemplified in Q3, where 20 organisations representing 74.07% of the organisations surveyed cut across 8 out of the 9 categories (or sectors). In contrast, the sectoral distribution across Q4, Q2, Q2 quads cut across a few sectors. This outcome supports the view in [2], which argued that the increasing level of ICT adoption in CI, has the potential to exacerbate high cyber risks profile amongst CI.

The quads of metrics (or Dependency Factor (DF)) shown in Figs. 5 and 6 charts demonstrate the characteristics of DF in terms of *Adoption, Integration* and *Automation*. Using the concept of ICT Dependency Quadrant (IDQ), the DF values of the metrics grouped in the quadrant can be comparatively analysed to provide useful insight into the growth of ICT in a particular sector or all sectors. The metric scores, which fall under Q3 quad-band represent 59.26% of the organisations. Similarly, 66.67% of the organisations' scores in Integration metric fall in Q3 band. This individual metric index is in contrast with the overall IDI of the organisations where 74.07% of the organisations fall in the Q3 band as can be derived from Table 6. However, it is important to note that the IDI score is a normalised composite value derived from the computation of the dependency metrics scores or DF based on the effect of weighted factors. Consequently, it can be added that the final IDI has compensating effects by the summation of the DFs. This metric compensating factor is chosen to balance the bias of individual metrics, which can affect the final IDI in terms of ICT dependency concerning cyber risks. The implication is that it can lead to a false sense of cyber risks. This factor suggests that organisations should drill down into individual metric scores to deepen the understanding of the various metric effects. Notwithstanding this, the weighted metric factors discussed in Table 2 balances the effect of metric bias and provides the basis for objective computation of IDI.

The trends clearly show that the organisations in Q1, Q2, and Q4 are fewer as opposed to Q3, which has 20 organisations cutting across many categories (or sectors). The trends are useful insights into the growth of ICT dependency, depicting a typically acceptable distribution curve in which most organisations are in Q3 quad, and fewer in Q4 quad, characterising the link between ICT dependency and cyber risks; implying that the growth of ICT dependency is directly proportional to the potential cyber risks as defined by IDQ. Consequently, as alluded in [33], the increasing ICT dependency

Table 7. Survey dataset showing dependency metrics and Dependency Factor (DF) scores

#	Code	Category	Adoption	Integration	Automation
1	VRJKP	Communications & Media	0.85	0.80	0.98
2	DUOHX	MDA	0.85	0.77	0.76
3	ULOWF	MDA	0.80	0.78	0.78
4	XNBPM	MDA	0.81	0.76	0.71
5	ZLPSV	MDA	0.79	0.81	0.68
6	UVEWC	Information Technology	0.74	0.74	0.72
7	ULMJG	MDA	0.79	0.78	0.66
8	THZDG	Security & Safety	0.75	0.67	0.76
9	AXKUN	MDA	0.90	0.73	0.60
10	PPJIW	MDA	0.70	0.80	0.64
11	NGDYE	Energy	0.72	0.74	0.65
12	ZREMB	Education	0.64	0.67	0.67
13	CROEX	Education	0.66	0.64	0.69
14	DDVPK	MDA	0.66	0.70	0.62
15	KCCEM	Energy	0.63	0.59	0.72
16	SVGVC	MDA	0.73	0.67	0.53
17	AGPXU	Education	0.66	0.61	0.59
18	FXBQV	Education	0.63	0.69	0.48
19	FXFMY	Energy	0.45	0.64	0.62
20	JXZNL	Health	0.65	0.64	0.48
21	GYNNY	Auxiliary Sectors	0.53	0.62	0.53
22	WVLGY	State	0.62	0.46	0.57
23	XQLAR	Security & Safety	0.76	0.59	0.34
24	NCHHK	MDA	0.53	0.50	0.40
25	FKVQH	Energy	0.54	0.63	0.28
26	LFKRM	MDA	0.51	0.51	0.06
27	VVZEN	MDAs	0.09	0.17	0.00

in critical infrastructure is also amplifying the risks exacerbated by the complexity of vulnerability and threat inherent in ICT. The pattern of growth depicted in Q3 reveals that no particular sector can be designated as more important (or critical) than the other but should take into cognizance the unique ICT growth in organisations since it is impractical amidst scarce resources to apply equal investment in mitigating the cyber risks.

Although it can be alluded to that significant research works have been done in ICT usage or dependency, our work differs pointedly in approach and results. Most

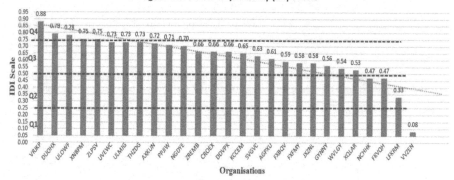

Fig. 4. Organisations IDI values and respective Quads

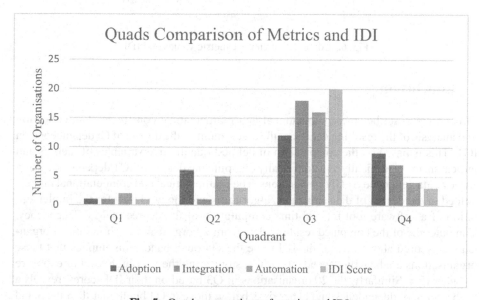

Fig. 5. Quads comparison of metrics and IDI

previous works focused on a qualitative approach, which lacked quantification of the actual degree of ICT dependency and can be ineffective in gauging potential cyber risks. Again, the quantitative measurement has the advantage of throwing more insights into different aspects (or metrics and indicators of ICT dependency) that can be effective in mitigating cyber risks based on empirical facts. Our approach has provided extensively both scientific and empirical tool that can help organisations monitor their ICT growth, and help CI regulators to comparatively gauge ICT dependency of CI organisations in a single view.

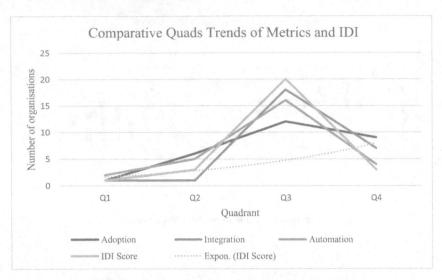

Fig. 6. Comparative view of metric values and IDI

7   Conclusion

This article describes the computational and mathematical constructs, data collection and analysis of the resulting data from the assessment of the degree of CI dependence on ICT. This is based on the computation of defined quantitative variables of metrics and indicators to scientifically and empirically compute the degree of ICT dependency using survey data generated by CI organisations. The mathematical and computational models helped in the design of data structures, algorithms and the workflow for the implementation of a software tool for real-time computation of the degree of ICT dependency. The outcome of the computed resulting data from 27 organisations shows that 3 organisations scored above 0.75 of the IDI to be the Q4 quad-band. This implies that these organisations are heavily dependent on ICT, suggesting the very high level of exposure to cyber risk. Similarly, the 20 organisations in Q3 based on their IDI scores, reveals a high degree of dependency and cyber risks below those in Q4 but higher than the 3 and 1 organisations in Q2 and Q1 respectively. This quantitative approach has revealed the link that can exist between ICT dependency metrics and inherent ICT risks due to the complexity of vulnerability and threat in the ICT ecosystem. Another key advantage of our solution is that a high IDI score portrays potential high cyber risks, which can be affected by the computed metric values (or DF). The potential metric bias is cushioned by the introduction of metric weighted factor to compensate for the effects of inherent vulnerability and threat in a particular metric. The assumption is that all metrics cannot have equal susceptibility to cyber risks. The measurement of the extent of a CI organisation's dependency on ICT, and in comparison, with other organisations is vitally important to how a nation can prioritise the CIIP since all CIs are unlikely to have the same characteristics and equal criticality. Consequently, CI organisations or regulatory bodies can apply our solution to scientifically and empirically evaluate their degree of ICT dependency continuously and in a repeatable transparent fashion. Applying the same repeatable and transparent tool undoubtedly can provide an unbiased assessment of the degree of ICT dependency of organisations across sectors. However, at present, general research in this area is still in its infancy, the drawback of our solution can stem from organisational bias in providing false data although this was mitigated during the survey by insisting on a minimum of 3 respondents per each organisation. Future will focus on how to mitigate the influence of organisational bias and negative contributing effect of the underlying metrics and indicators.

Acknowledgement. This research is supported by the TETFund National Research Fund (NRF) research grant TETF/DR&D/CE/NRF/UNI/KEFFI/VOL.1/B5 to Nasarawa State University, Keffi, Nigeria.

References

1. Banerjee, J., Das, A., Sen, A., Science, C.: A survey of interdependency models for critical infrastructure networks. Phys. Soc-ph. (2017). https://doi.org/10.3233/978-1-61499-391-9-1
2. Kure, H., Islam, S., Razzaque, M.: An integrated cyber security risk management approach for a cyber-physical system. Appl. Sci. **8**(6), 898 (2018). https://doi.org/10.3390/app8060898
3. USA Patriot Act. USA PATRIOT Act Additional Reauthorizing Amendments Act of 2006 (S. 2271) 2001 (2005), 1–6. http://www.fas.org/sgp/crs/intel/RS22384.pdf
4. Izuakor, C., White, R.: Critical Infrastructure Protection XI. 2017 512, 27-41. https://doi.org/10.1007/978-3-319-70395-4
5. Canzani, E.: Dynamic interdependency models for cybersecurity of critical infrastructures (2017)
6. Mbanaso, U., Kulugh, V., Musa, H., Aimufua, G.: Conceptual framework for the assessment of the degree of dependency of critical national infrastructure on ICT in Nigeria. In: 15th International Conference on Electronic Computers and Computations, Abuja, Nigeria: IEEE Xplore, vol. 15 (2019). https://doi.org/10.1109/ICECCO48375.2019.9043230
7. Rehak, D., Senovsky, P., Hromada, M., Lovecek, T., Novotny, P.: PT US CR. Int. J. Crit. Infrastruct. Prot. **22**, 125–138 (2018). https://doi.org/10.1016/j.ijcip.2018.06.004
8. Argonne National Laboratory. Analysis of Critical Infrastructure Dependencies and Interdependencies, vol. 15/4 (2015). http://www.osti.gov/scitech/
9. Dobson, S., Hutchison, D., Mauthe, A., Schaeffer-Filho, A., Smith, P., Sterbenz, J.: Self-organization and resilience for networked systems: design principles and open research issues (2019), 1–16. https://doi.org/10.1109/JPROC.2019.2894512
10. Petit, F., Bassett, G., Buehring, W.A., Whitfield, R.G.: Resilience Measurement Index: An Indicator of Critical Infrastructure Resilience, April (2013), 70. www.osti.gov/bridge
11. Pursiainen, C.: Critical infrastructure resilience: a Nordic model in the making? Int. J. Disaster Risk Reduct. **27**, 1 (2017). https://doi.org/10.1016/j.ijdrr.2017.08.006
12. Willke, B.J.: A critical information infrastructure protection approach to multinational cyber security events. Carnegie Mellon Univ., September 2007. http://www.enisa.europa.eu/activities/cert/events/files/ENISA_best_practices_for_ciip_Willke.pdf
13. Mbanaso, U., Kulugh, V., Musa, H., Aimufua, G.: Conceptual framework for the assessment of the degree of dependency of critical national infrastructure on ICT in Nigeria. In: Proceedings of 15th International Conference on Electronics, Computer and Computation (ICECCO), Abuja, Nigeria: IEEE Xplore, vol. 15 (2019). https://doi.org/10.1109/ICECCO48375.2019.9043230

14. Bibao-Osorio, B., Dutta, S., Lanvin, B.: Global information technology report 2014: rewards and risks of big data (2014). http://reports.weforum.org/global-information-technology-report-2014/
15. Setola, R., Luiijf, E., Theocharidou, M.: Managing the complexity of critical infrastructures. Manag Complexityof Crit InfrastructuresA Model Simul Approach. 90(Ci), 1–18 (2017). https://doi.org/10.1007/978-3-319-51043-9
16. Taylor, P., Zand, F., Solaimani, S., et al.: A role-based typology of information technology: model development and assessment. Role-Based Typology Inf. Technol., 37–41 (2015). https://doi.org/10.1080/10580530.2015.1018770
17. Fekete, A.: Common criteria for the assessment of critical infrastructures. Int. Disaster Risk Sci. 2(1), 15–24 (2011). https://doi.org/10.1007/s13753-011-0002-y
18. Bloomfield, R.E., Popov, P., Salako, K., Stankovic, V., Wright, D.: Preliminary interdependency analysis: an approach to support critical-infrastructure risk-assessment. Reliab. Eng. Syst. Saf. 2017(167), 198–217 (2015). https://doi.org/10.1016/j.ress.2017.05.030
19. Robinson, M., Jones, K., Janicke, H., Maglaras, L.: An introduction to cyber peacekeeping. J. Netw. Comput. Appl. 114 (2018). https://doi.org/10.1016/j.jnca.2018.04.010
20. Krepinevich, A.F.: Cyber warfare a "nuclear option"? Cent. Strateg. Budg. Assessments (2012)
21. Izuakor, C., White, R.: Critical infrastructure asset identification: policy, methodology and gap analysis. IFIP Adv. Inf. Commun. Technol. 485, 27–41 (2016). https://doi.org/10.1007/978-3-319-48737-3_2
22. Buldyrev, S.V., Parshani, R., Paul, G., Stanley, H.E., Havlin, S.: Catastrophic cascade of failures in interdependent networks. Nature 464(7291), 1025–1028 (2010). https://doi.org/10.1038/nature08932
23. Kundhavai, K.R., Sridevi, S.: International journal of computer science and mobile computing IoT and Big Data-the current and future technologies: a review. Int. J. Comput. Sci. Mob. Comput. 5(1), 10–14 (2016). www.ijcsmc.com
24. Theohary, C.A., Rollins, J.W.: Cyberwarfare and cyberterrorism: in brief. Congr. Res. Serv. (2015). www.crs.gov
25. Schreier, F.: On cyberwarfare. DCAF Horiz 2015 Work Pap No.7 (2015)
26. Saloky, T., Šeminský, J.: Artificial intelligence and machine learning applied to cybersecurity. IEEE. Conflu., pp. 1–18 (2017). http://uniobuda.hu/conferences/SAMI2005/SALOKY.pdf
27. Tatar, U., Gokce, Y., Gheorghe, A.: Strategic cyber defense: a multidisciplinary perspective. In: NATO Advanced Research Workshop on a Framework for a Military Cyber Defense Strategy (2017)
28. Galinec, D., Steingartner, W.: Combining cybersecurity and cyber defense to achieve cyber resilience. In: 2017 IEEE 14th International Scientific Conference on Informatics Combining, pp. 87–93 (2017)
29. Almeida, A., Técnico, I.S.: A Multi-Criteria Methodology for the Identification & Ranking of Critical Infrastructures, pp. 1–10. Instituto Superior Técnico, Lisbon, Port Abstr. (2008)
30. Baboo, S.S., Megalai, S.M.: Cyber forensic investigation and exploration on cloudcomputing environment. Glob. J. Comput. Sci. Technol. B Cloud Distrib. 15(1) (2015)
31. WEF.: Industrial Internet of Things: Unleashing the Potential of Connected Products and Services, p. 40. World Economic Forum (2015). https://doi.org/10.1111/hcre.12119
32. Lee, R.M., Assante, M.J., Conway, T.: Analysis of the Cyber Attack on the Ukrainian Power Grid. Washington DC (2016). www.eisac.com
33. Donzelli, P., Setola, R., Tucci, S.: Identifying and evaluating critical infrastructures - a goal-driven dependability analysis framework. In: Proceedings of the International Conference on Communications in Computing, CIC 2004, 21–24 June 2004, Las Vegas, Nevada, USA (2004)

34. Anderson, R.N.: U. S. -Canada Power System Outage Task Force Final Report on the August 14, 2003 Blackout in the United States and Canada : Causes and Recommendations, (August 2004) (2019)
35. Seppänen, H., Luokkala, P., Zhang, Z., Torkki, P., Virrantaus, K.: Critical infrastructure vulnerability—a method for identifying the infrastructure service failure interdependencies Hannes. Int. J. Crit. Infrastruct. Prot. (2018). https://doi.org/10.1016/j.ijcip.2018.05.002
36. Tweneboah-Koduah, S., Buchanan, W.J.: Security risk assessment of critical infrastructure systems: a comparative study. Comput. J. **61**(9), 1389–1406 (2018). https://doi.org/10.1093/comjnl/bxy002
37. WEF: The Global Information Technology Report 2016, (2016). http://www3.weforum.org/docs/GITR2016/WEF_GITR_Full_Report.pdf%0A
38. UNCTAD.: Measuring the Impacts of Information and Communication Technology for Development (2011)
39. ITU.: Global Cybersecurity Index (GCI) 2018 (2018). D-STR-GCI.01–2018-PDF-E.pdf
40. European Commission: Final Report On Study on Critical Dependencies of Energy, Finance and Transport Infrastructures on ICT Infrastructure On Behalf of the European Commission DG Justice, Freedom and Security (2009)
41. Voeller, J.G., Black, P.E., Scarfone, K., Souppaya, M.: Cyber Security Metrics and Measures. Wiley Handb Sci Technol Homel Secur. (2008). https://doi.org/10.1002/978047008 7923.hhs440
42. Robert, G., Greenhalgh, T., MacFarlane, F., Peacock, R.: Organisational Factors Influencing Technology Adoption and Assimilation in the NHS: A Systematic Literature Review: Report for the National Institute for Health Research Service Delivery and Organisation Programme (2009)
43. Atkin, D., Chaudhry, A., Chaudry, S., Khandelwal, A.K., Verhoogen, E.: Organizational barriers to technology adoption: evidence from soccer-ball producers in Pakistan. Q. J. Econ. **132**(3), 1101–1164 (2017). https://doi.org/10.1093/qje/qjx010
44. UNCTAD.: Measuring the Impacts of Information and Communication Technology for Development. New York (2011)
45. United Nations: Core ICT Indicators:Partnership on Measuring ICT for Development (2005). www.itu.int/ITU-D/ict/partnership/material/CoreICTIndicators.pdf
46. Chew, E., Swanson, M., Stine, K., Bartol, N., Brown, A., Robinson, W.: Performance Measurement Guide for Information Security, pp. 800–55. NIST Spec Publ. Revis July 1 2008
47. NITDA.: Nigeria E-Government Interoperability Framework (Ne-GIF) National Information Technology Development Agency (NITDA) (2019). http://nitda.gov.ng/wp-content/uploads/2018/05/data-interoperability-standards.pdf

Mapping of Security Issues and Concerns in Cloud Computing with Compromised Security Attributes

Alok Raj[1]([✉]) [ID], Nitin Jain[2] [ID], and Surendra Singh Chauhan[3] [ID]

[1] Panjab University, Chandigarh, India
[2] Chandigarh University, Mohali, India
[3] Pratap University, Jaipur, India

Abstract. In the ongoing years with the headway of innovation, cloud computing has gotten colossal mainstream among organizations, aggressors just as people because of a few favorable circumstances however the fundamental advantages being versatility, flexibility, unwavering quality, high computation power, convenience and cost-proficient as these hugely advantage all the parties in question. Be that as it may, with this exponential increment cloud computing environments have become a high potential target for the attackers as they have witnessed some drawbacks in terms of security and data privacy. One of the fundamental reasons behind for cloud computing environments being a gold dig for attackers is the presence of unencrypted data on these platforms which are indexed and along these lines effortlessly found. This paper talks about the risks, challenges and security concerns present in a cloud computing environment that affects both the cloud service providers and the clients. This paper has talked about the issues and concerns from an end-user perspective as well as from a business viewpoint also. In this way these risks, challenges and security concerns end up being compelling and proficient in deciding the general security of a cloud domain as it covers practically all the specialized issues just as well as standardization, regulations and supervising perspectives identified with it. The challenges have likewise prompted development opportunities that must be tackled. As cloud computing environment is an extremely unpredictable and dynamic as for conventional computing environment, so the customary security practices and arrangements does not delineate in cloud situations. There are unbounded potential outcomes of development in cloud computing which cannot be inconspicuous because of security and data privacy issues so these risks, challenges, and security concerns must be tended to.

Keywords: Cloud security · Cloud security challenges · Cloud security issues · Information security · Data privacy · Security attributes · Cloud security concern

1 Introduction

Recent years have seen that a greater part of associations is encountering digital assaults running from two times per year to once at regular intervals. The digital assaults contrast

R. Agrawal et al. (Eds.): ICCEDE 2020, CCIS 1436, pp. 24–40, 2021.
https://doi.org/10.1007/978-3-030-84842-2_2

regarding extent, effect, strategy or method of assault, and dangers related with them. The most arranged associations on the planet cannot deny the danger of digital assaults. As organizations and associations are moving to online stages like cloud condition and developing their organizations quickly over the web, they are setting themselves up to confront significantly more digital assaults in the coming years. Significant explanation behind this move is to satisfy their equipment asset necessities absent a lot of starting venture because of pay as you use membership administrations gave by the cloud specialist co-ops and furthermore because of the way that putting away information over cloud stages makes it effectively available from anyplace around the globe and there is an extremely less likelihood of information misfortune due to as replication factor for put away information in cloud condition (Fig. 1).

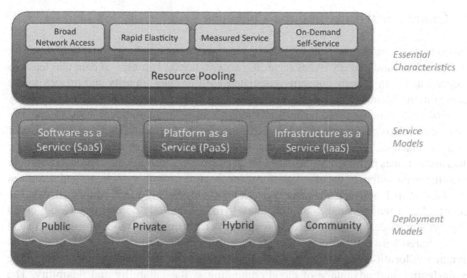

Fig. 1. Cloud Computing- NIST Visual Model (Source: https://www.researchgate.net/public ation/241195178/figure/fig2/AS:400869486022664@1472586141957/NIST-Visual-Model-of-Cloud-Computing-a-Service-Models-Cloud-computing-can-be-classified.png)

National Institute of Standards and Technology (NIST) defines Cloud Computing as "Cloud Computing is a model for enabling ubiquitous, convenient, on-demand network access to a shared pool of configurable computing resources (e.g. networks, servers, storage, application and services) that can be rapidly provisioned and released with minimal management effort or service provider interaction" [1]. Frameworks and Information Security and Data Privacy is a significant concern when organizations and associations consider relocating to the cloud. According to ISO/IEC 27000:2013, Information Security is a resource for any association which like some other resource has its incentive regarding Confidentiality, Integrity and Availability. This investigation is identified with the information handled, sent, and put away through and inside the cloud condition and the security danger and concerns identified with it. Respectability of information in cloud stages assumes an essential function in the reception of cloud however it doesn't guarantee the hidden preparing strategies for information handling along these lines protecting the exactness and culmination of information can't be guaranteed in such cases. Secrecy of information in cloud stages remains the significant concern, particularly on account of network cloud and public cloud as the information can be undermined because of the issues looked by different associations sharing the cloud stage that the other association civic chairman may not know about. Apart from Confidentiality, Integrity and Availability, the use of virtualization (hardware-level virtualization or hypervisor or bare-metal virtualization as well as software-level virtualization) and nested virtualization in cloud platforms have several security risks associated with it. This paper deals with the risks, issues, and challenges in a cloud computing environment.

2 Cloud Security Issues and Concerns

Cloud services have several benefits and advantages associated with it but still there are some security and privacy issues regarding access, use and storage of data that leads to security and data privacy concerns associated with it. Data security and privacy in the cloud environment is a major concern and strong cryptography is not the one and only powerful solution that could be implemented [3]. Some of the major areas of research in a cloud computing environment is related to security concerns and issues includes loss of control, data loss, service disruption, etc. Undoubtedly it isn't an easy task to secure the data and services provided by the cloud service providers through the cloud environment and ensure the safety of the cloud platform due to a large number of clients and resources involved. This leads to multi-tenancy in cloud environment to help reduce costs to the clients. Multi-tenancy makes public cloud, hybrid cloud and community cloud, cloud deployment models possible because while implementing these models' resources need to be shared between individual clients as well as organizations. For this, proper and dynamic allocation of resources needs to be done as per the requirements because the main feature and advantage of cloud computing is its scalability and flexibility. The cloud service providers as well as the clients face several challenges on their respective ends but their main concern remains in the areas related to cloud security which includes the availability of resources, data privacy and security, data processing policies, and the terms and conditions provided by the cloud service providers and accepted by the clients. But the first fine line of defense lies in the implementation of cloud service so that a safe and secure cloud computing environment can be established.

Some of the prominent security issues and concerns in a cloud environment are as follows:

2.1 Management Interface Compromise

Services provided via cloud environment are accessible and delivered over the Internet remotely and the resources are also accessible and managed over the Internet to make any required configuration changes [8]. Thus, access of services by any unintended third-party can lead to malicious activities, non-optimal use of resources, and other risks associated with it [9, 25]. Account and Service Hijacking is the easiest way to compromise the management console. Stolen credentials or weak credentials can lead to account or service hijacking. Account hijacking can be done with the help of various phishing techniques, cyber frauds, bad credential management, insecure handling of credentials, etc. Service hijacking can be done by the exploitation of software vulnerabilities, untimely updates of services, not changing services defaults, or use of outdated services. If an account or service has been hijacked, then the attacker can access critical data and disrupt services. Remote access and Web Browser Vulnerabilities such as Remote File Inclusion (RFI), directory traversals, remote code execution and other such vulnerabilities can increase the risks [20].

2.2 Multi-tenancy

Shared access of computational resources (i.e. hardware, software, or both), also referred to as multitenancy is one of the major threats to data security and privacy in a cloud infrastructure environment. Since, multiple clients or precisely, multiple end users are sharing the same computational resources like processor, memory, storage, etc., so, it arises a security concern and related risks to not only a single client but multiple clients that are sharing the same computational resources [9]. In such cases there is always a higher probability of risk related to private and sensitive data accidentally leaking or being disclosed to other clients [6, 7, 10]. The vulnerabilities and exploits that targets multitenant infrastructure can be exceptionally risky because one loophole in the system of any of the client can let other client or hacker to have access to all the sensitive as well as potential insensitive data present in that environment [30]. Thus, in case of a multi-tenancy a hacker tries to compromise any of the multiple clients to gain access to the environment of one customer which can eventually help him gain access to the complete environment.

2.3 Elasticity

The major challenge faced in cloud environment with respect to elasticity is the ability to provide fine grained access and predefined security controls. Elasticity in a cloud environment is limited by its capacity. Thus, the cloud service providers have to impose strict limitations on the amount of resources that will be provided to one customer else it can lead to resource unavailability that can be caused by computer attack or network attacks affecting the complete cloud environment rather than a particular customer [12]. More elasticity will provide to more flexibility to import or export data in case of a multi-tenancy cloud environment.

2.4 Vendor Lock-in

In the recent times, there is extraordinarily little option available for the customer to have application, data and service portability in the cloud environment. Any customer cannot easily migrate their services between cloud environments managed by different cloud service providers or cloud brokers as interoperability of application and data is very difficult along with the presence of proprietary services by different cloud service providers [8, 20]. The main reasons for this are the lack of standard technologies and solutions in a cloud environment and lack of completeness and transparency in terms of use [12]. In SaaS lock-in situation, if the cloud service provider is not providing a way to export the data automatically in a standard format then the customer must do it manually at regular intervals in order to access the data in other platforms. In PaaS, a lock-in situation occurs at the API layer as different cloud service providers offers different API's. In IaaS, a lock-in situation depends upon the specific infrastructure services availed by the customer from the cloud service provider.

2.5 Isolation Failure

Sharing of resources when on a cloud environment with almost no access to physical devices and no information about the underlying implementation is itself a security threat [8]. Several problems occur when isolation failure in storage devices where critical data and information is stored [23]. Other major areas of isolation failure concerns include memory and routing information [20]. Attacking on hypervisors and cloud environment are much more difficult for attackers and therefore often less than traditional OS but still in case of isolation failure, failure in resources of one customer and disrupt the services of all the customers sharing that resources. Isolation of web-apps, database servers, virtual data-center environments are also the major concerns. Isolation failure can lead to guest-hopping-attacks and other such attacks.

2.6 Insecure or Incomplete Data Deletion

In a cloud environment, when a customer deletes a cloud resource, true or real wiping of data may not occur [8]. This may be possible as the disk may also contain data from other customers or copies of the data to be deleted may not be temporarily available due to unavailability of resources at real-time [12]. Also, in a cloud environment, the resources are shared and reused. So, there are chances of retrieval of critical data by other intended customer which was not the case with dedicated hardware. Also, data security and privacy policies like secure disposal and reuse of equipment is followed or not is known by the client unless and until the cloud service provider proves that it is compliant towards any industry standard.

2.7 Network Attacks

DDoS attacks, Port Scanning, Flooding Attack can lead to service disruption for the customer as well as added cost for the use of cloud resources [12, 16, 24]. Other network-based threats such as DNS attack, Sniffer attack, Prefix Hijacking, IP Address reuse, IP Spoofing, Fragmentation Attack, Deep Packet Inspection, Active and Passive Eavesdropping also possesses high risk and threat [26, 27]. Cloud service provider charges the customers based on the use of resources. Network attacks have a deep impact on the bandwidth and can increase the use of network resources drastically thus adding added costs to the customer apart from disruption of services that leads to economic as well as business losses.

2.8 High Availability and DR Readiness

Proper implementation and readiness of Disaster Recovery Planning (DRP) by the cloud service provider and readiness Business Continuity Planning (BCP) for the cloud customer is an important part of risk assessment and management that should be tended to [12].

2.9 Access Control

Implementation of proper accessing controls such as fine-grained access control policies or coarse-grained access control policies along with role-based access control and rule-based access control to provide audited, restricted or controlled access efficiently and effectively to maintain an easily manageable and privilege distribution mechanism remains a major challenge in a cloud environment [12]. Centralized access control mechanisms have its own advantages but other authorization mechanisms such as Mandatory Access Control (MAC), Discretionary Access Control (DAC), Role-Based Access Control (RBAC) and Attribute-Based Access Control (ABAC) should also be considered [27].

2.10 Authentication and Authorization

Deployment of a proper Identity and Access Management Solution is a major challenge in a cloud environment. Cloud Providers (CP) use services from identity providers (IdP) that issues identities or credentials to the users, while a relying party (RP) depends on the Identity Provider to check the user credentials before it allows users access to the cloud services. This approach is implemented by most of the cloud service providers but has usability and security challenges associated with it [21]. Cloud service providers provide Identity-as-a-Service (IDaaS) to its customers [22]. IDaaS requires several core characteristics to be deployed as expected regardless of the cloud service provider vendor. Multi-factor authentication is available but not mandated by most of the cloud service providers [27].

2.11 Defense-in-Depth

Defense-in-Depth covers the security policies and controls applicable at each layer to ensure systems and information security and data privacy. Ensuring the proper implementation of defense-in-depth is a major challenge in a cloud computing environment [20]. Cloud Security Alliance structures a cloud environment in seven different layers [6]:

- The Facility Layer (physical security of physical resources by restricting physical access to cloud environment)
- The Network Layer (maintenance, monitoring and auditing network flow diagram)
- The Hardware Layer (monitoring and proper allocation of resources)
- The OS Layer (deployment of OS with proper security policy and configuration)

- The Middleware Layer (secure communication between various systems within cloud environment with the use of encryption)
- The Application Layer (secure coding and secure software development of application that will be provided the public as a service)
- The User Layer (monitor access pattern for malicious user)

  - Web Based Application Cloud User – access information in cloud environment in insecure environment
  - Member of Customer Organization User – access information with security policy.

2.12 Misuse and Iniquitous Use of Cloud Computing Environment

Cyber criminals like spammers, hackers, and fraudsters take advantage of cloud computing by using the resources for crime ware-as-a-service to fulfil their computation needs or to initiate and launch various attacks like Distributed Denial-of-Service (DDoS), password decryption, hash cracking, etc. [6, 7, 10, 25]. Resources on a cloud environment can reduce the time taken for cracking passwords or breaking hashes. Simpler registration process, easier allocation of resources and on-demand and on-the-go resource and service allocation i.e. scalability as per the needs and requirements makes it easier for the cyber criminals to fulfil their computational needs and resources at a very nominal cost. Cyber-criminals use cloud environment to offer malwares such as viruses, botnets, Trojans, keyloggers, etc. on subscription by the use of forums and hosting the website and uploading the malwares in secured archive files over the cloud platform from where the users can download them after paying for the subscription via cryptocurrency or online multi-currency wallets. Hackers now don't have to invest on computing resources and bandwidth, but they can use resources and bandwidth provided by the cloud providers and even provide it as a service. They can configure cloud machines and provide it for crimeware-as-a-service on rental and this threat is increasing. Let us consider the example of a malware. For a polymorphic virus, the polymorphic engine needn't to reside within the virus code itself, but it could be remotely stored on a server. In such case, the virus can mutate remotely via a command over HTTP or HTTPS [5] or any other protocol on a covert channel for which the malware has been configured. Some of the popular use cases of crimeware-as-a-service are [4]:

Hacking-as-a-Service. The Shadow Broker hacker and threat actor group that was behind the WannaCry ransomware attacks announced in 2017 that it will let it customers access exploits, zero-days, and hacking tools that they stole from the U.S. government on a monthly subscription of $23,000 per month.

Do-it-Yourself. Exploits are being sold as per market demands by increasing costs - Exploit kits like Angler exploit and Neutrino Kit are made available to the customers on a SaaS basis in black markets. The price of Neutrino kit doubled nearly overnight to $7,000 from $3,500, when the Angler exploit kit disappeared from the black market.

IoT Botnet on Rental (Botnet-as-a-Service). One can rent the Command and Control Centre of IoT botnets for performing a DDoS attack. A resource on cloud computing by any of the cloud service provider can be developed overtime to become the CCC that can then be rented to carry a DDoS attack using IoT device such as smart TV, smart refrigerator and other such devices as bot which were previously compromised. Apart from IoT botnets, general system botnets are also available to the customers.

Designer-Malware-as-a-Service. Diamond Fox is an example of such modularized malware service that offers more than thousands of different options, fronted with a highly professional and user-friendly management panel to generate and deploy malwares.

Ransomware-as-a-Service. The creators of such services ask no up-front fee but they take a 20% share in the profit for any ransom paid by victims to its users. Tox and Cerber are such examples.

Phishing-as-Service. Some uses cloud computing platforms to offer VIP subscriptions to a marketplace with phished credentials with average subscription costs between $0.15 and $15.39 each.

Backdoor-as-a-Service. Such services are generally provided by hacking groups. These groups compromise systems and plant backdoor for continued remote access using Remote Access Trojan (RAT) and other such programs. They then sell the access to these systems to the customers.

Fraud-as-a-Service. This service provides its customers with replicated legitimate services which looks like legitimate offerings that can be used by the customers to trick the victims.

Spam-as-a-Service. These services provide their customers the ability to send spam e-mail or messages at a very cheap cost where the providers can charge on hourly basis or on subscription.

2.13 Unidentified Risk Report and Service Level Agreement

When an organization is using any cloud service model, the organization is not directly interacting with the hardware resources and software interaction is very less [6, 7, 10]. This leads to "Lack of Appropriate Governance" where there exist several vulnerabilities depending on the organization's business and the organization's security and compliance are at stake which affects its assets and eventually its business [9, 20]. The major drawbacks are found in the terms of use agreement and the service-level agreements where the cloud service providers states that they have no responsibility or liability over the customer's data whereas in some cases the cloud service provider can have complete control over the data. At times, proper security defense mechanisms and standards are not a part of the SLA [12]. Also, the customer or the client must seek for proper clauses in the SLA that defines the responsibilities of both parties in case of data loss or leakage and the extent of permission that the client has over the main underlying cloud infrastructure to deploy a forensics expert for carrying out the process of digital forensics and collecting electronic evidences in case of any data breach. The main reason behind this is that the consumers don't have a clear insight of the cloud providers terms and conditions i.e. security metrics are not included in the Service-Level Agreements (SLAs) [29].

2.14 Compliance Risks

Using or providing services in a cloud environment requires certain compliance i.e. industry wide accepted standard or regulatory requirements which cannot be achieved by every single organization [19]. This may be due to several reasons some of which being that the cloud service provider cannot provide evidence of their own compliance or the cloud service provider doesn't give the permission for the conduction of an audit to the client which requires physical on-site audit as well as network audit, which is mostly in case of a public cloud and community cloud [8, 20].

2.15 Location Transparency

Some cloud service providers don't provide the exact and actual geographical location of the resources which contains the data of the customer [14, 24]. This is a major with the resources where backups are stored. This has risks associated with it for the businesses. This also includes risks associate with changes of jurisdiction and licensing. Location transparency matters the most for data privacy and security as location transparency determines that which data protection act will be applicable such as General Data Protection Regulation (GDPR) [18], California Consumer Privacy Act (CCPA) [17].

2.16 Insider Attacks/Wicked Insiders

Malicious Attacks originating from within the organization providing cloud service. Malicious insiders are the biggest threat in cloud computing environment that cannot be predicted [19, 25, 29]. Disgruntled employees can easily have access to data if proper access controls measures have not been implemented [6–8, 10]. If the employees have access to the physical resources, then no security controls can prevent the data leakage or theft except full-disk encryption in some cases where storage devices are stolen. Insider attacks can occur from both customer organization or the provider organization as well as by ex-employees or external contractors or business partners including third-party service providers and can cause substantial damage [20, 27, 28].

2.17 Accountability and Auditing

Auditing a cloud environment is also a major challenge in public cloud infrastructure that has operations, business and information security risks associated with it. Accountability directly affects the AAA services which lead to difficulties in implementing a proper information security model.

2.18 Use of Proper Secure Protocols and Security Standards

The cloud service provider should use secure protocols and security standards to minimize the risk. For establishing and maintaining a secure and protected environment that **provides systems and information security as well as data privacy, some specific steps** are taken by implementing the below mentioned cloud related standards and methods [13].

DLP, TLS v1.2 or Higher, HTTPS Protocols. These protocols should be used for data in transit to main the confidentiality of data during transit i.e. to achieve data loss prevention.

Security Assertion Markup Language (SAML). This standard should be implemented for secure communication between online partners as SAML allows identity providers (IdP) like Google, Facebook, etc. to pass authorization credentials to cloud service providers (SP) to implement secure authentication services and thus reducing business and information security risks. SAML uses SAM, XML, HTTPS and SOAP protocols to implement single sign-on for enterprise users [23].

Open Authentication (OAuth). OAuth simplifies the authorization process by granting access to data, services, platforms, etc. without having the need to deal with the original authentication packets. Protected and sensitive data can be communicated securely by using this method. It doesn't actually share the password or password data in any form, but it uses authorization tokens to prove an identity between client and service providers. It is an authentication protocol that allows the client to approve that one application is interacting with another application on the client's behalf without giving away or sharing the client's actual password. It was introduced to make privacy enhancement by removing the users' requirement of sharing their passwords with any third-party applications. OAuth uses JSON and HTTPS protocol to implement API authorization between applications.

OpenID. OpenID helps in authentication i.e. it helps to prove the identity of the user. It is an open-source decentralized protocol used to implement single-sign-on (SSO) method. It was introduced to provide federated authentication, i.e., a third-party can authenticate the users for the service provider by using accounts or identities that the user already have with the third-party. OpenID uses XRDS and HTTPS protocol to implement single-sign-on for clients.

2.19 Virtualization Risks

In a cloud environment, virtualization poses some potential risks to data as they perform their own cycles in different stages [29]. The major risk associated with virtualization is the compromising of the hypervisor itself. If a hypervisor is vulnerable, then it can become a primary target by the attackers and can lead to the compromise of the whole environment and all the data of all the customers [12]. Another severe risk associated with the use of the virtualization is the proper and secure allocation as well as de-allocation of resources [9]. If the allocated memory is not cleared or wiped before re-allocation, then the data can be recovered and thus exposed. Cloud service providers are now moving towards containerization-as-a-service (CaaS) and now they are implementing containerization with the help of Docker and Kubernetes instead of virtualization in cases where applicable, but containerization has its own advantages, disadvantages and security concerns. Security is a major concern in virtualized environment because virtualization adds more points of entry and more interconnection complexity [30]. VM rollback attack, VM escape attack and Cross-Virtual-Machine Side-Channel attacks are the most common types of attacks.

2.20 Secure Patches and Updates

Deployment of secure patches and updates in a timely manner by the cloud service provider carries a risk associated with it. Critical patches and updates carry the highest risk factor as it can lead to exposure of vulnerabilities [12].

2.21 Data Protection and Data Privacy

In a cloud computing environment, it is not ensured that the cloud service providers are following the data handling practices according to the laws and legislations as some cloud service providers don't disclose this information [24]. There are two states where the data in a cloud environment must be protected; Protection of Data at Rest refers to the protection of data stored within the cloud environment and Protection of Data in Transit refers to protection of data while it is moving in (uploading), being processed within the cloud environment, or going out (downloading) [9]. Data in transit can contain sensitive and critical data like Personal Identifiable Information and credentials. Data in rest can also contain sensitive and critical data stored in databases or in the system. Also, physical control over the data is also a major data protection challenge in a cloud environment. Storage-as-a-Service (SaaS) is also a major service provided by cloud service providers which is directly dependent on data protection. So, data protection especially of Personally Identifiable Information (PII) and sensitive information is a major concern when availing cloud services [24].

2.22 Data Crash and Data Loss

Data crash or data loss refers to the deletion or alteration of data without the presence of any backups [12]. It also includes loss of encryption keys, exposure of sensitive data, unauthorized access of data, unavailability of data, insecure deletion of data, availability of incomplete data, unavailability or unlinking of a record from a large environment, sudden disruption of any running service causing the temporary but sensitive data to be inaccessible and breakdown of storage devices without any available backups [6, 7, 9, 10, 12]. There issues can easily occur in cloud environment if the client if not experienced enough in using and handling cloud services.

2.23 Data Interception

Segmentation and distribution of data in transit occurs in a cloud environment that didn't occur in case of private computing resources. Thus, security threats such as sniffing, spoofing, third-party attacks, credential replay attacks, passive man-in-a-middle attack have higher risks due to fragility and vulnerability in computing resources [9, 12, 15].

2.24 Proper Use of Strong Cryptographic Functions

The cloud service provider should use strong cryptographic methods like RSA 2048-bit or higher, ECC (Elliptic Curve Cryptography), Multivariate Cryptography, Lattice-based Cryptography as encryption algorithms and SHA-512, RIPEMD-320, and Whirlpool as hashing algorithms while designing and implementing a cloud environment [12]. The cryptographic algorithms should be strong enough so as to maintain the integrity of data and avoid man-in-the-middle (MITM) attacks.

2.25 Insecure API

Cloud service providers providing IaaS uses APIs to allow clients to handle and interact with cloud platform. In PaaS Cloud Service Model, the API's deployed by the cloud service provider allows the customers to develop new applications. SaaS service providers offers API calls to read data records. Thus, the cloud service providers must ensure that data privacy and security is integrated and audited into their service models and API security and vulnerability assessment and testing must be done before its integration [6, 7, 10, 23]. The users also must be aware of the security risks that can be caused due to bad handling of these APIs [25]. The cloud service provider must also ensure that the API is compatible with the underling service. The problems in API's can lead to lock-in at different layer in different cloud service models.

2.26 Account, Service, Traffic and Session/TCP Hijacking

Stolen credentials are usually used to carry out account or service hijacking. Social engineering attacks especially phishing attacks, cyber-frauds, and exploitation of software vulnerabilities are the most common examples that can be used for hijacking. Confidentiality, Integrity and Availability of services can be affected if an attacker gains access to critical areas of cloud computing environment by hijacking [6, 7, 10, 12, 25, 27, 29]. Session/TCP hijacking also remains a common threat in cloud environments.

2.27 Web Based Attacks

Web-based attacks like Injection Attacks, XSS Attack, CSRF Attack, Wrapping Attack, lack of proper input validation, Cookie Poisoning, Captcha Breaking, etc. are also one of the major threats in a cloud computing environment [12, 26, 27]. In a cloud computing environment, most of the services are provided through a web-based platform so web-based attacks are most common and can lead to initialization of multiple threat vectors which can result in a targeted attack. Web application vulnerability scanning and mapping discovered vulnerability with National Vulnerability Database (NVD) and Common Weakness Enumeration (CWE) is the most common way to discover web-based vulnerabilities [13].

2.28 Privilege Escalation

Privilege escalation is a major threat that poses a major security threat. This can allow an unprivileged user to gain sufficient privileged access to compromise or destroy the entire system [27].

3 Observations and Findings

Security issues need to be mapped with security attributes to determine the impact of the issue along with the level of concern that is required to resolve the issue. For every security concern, the compromised security attributes can be divided into major and minor attributes. The security effects of major compromised security attributes are witnessed instantly where the security effects of minor compromised security attributes can be witnessed in the long run and can often be un-noticed. The following Table 1 shows the mapping of security issues with compromised security issues.

Table 1. Mapping of Security Issues and Concerns with Compromised Security Attributes

Security Issues and Concerns	Major Compromised Security Attributes	Minor Compromised Security Attributes
Management Interface Compromise	Confidentiality, Privacy, Robustness	Integrity, Reliability, Atomicity
Multi-Tenancy	Confidentiality, Integrity, Availability, Privacy, Robustness	Audit, Compliance, Accountability
Elasticity	Throughput, Confidentiality, Diligence	Availability, Integrity
Isolation Failure	Availability, Integrity	Confidentiality, Authenticity
Vendor Lock-In	Availability, Compliance, Transparency, Robustness	Confidentiality
Insecure or Incomplete Data Deletion	Confidentiality, Robustness	Privacy, Availability
Network Attacks	Reliability, Integrity, Availability, Confidentiality, Privacy	Trust, Accountability
High Availability and DR Readiness (if not provided)	Availability, Trust, Robustness	Deferment
Access Control	Authentication, Authorization, Identity	Trust, Accountability
Authentication and Authorization	Reliability, Integrity, Privacy, Trust	Consistency, Accountability
Defence-in-Depth	Complete Information Security and Data Privacy Failure	Complete Information Security and Data Privacy Failure
Misuse and Iniquitous use of Cloud Computing Environment	Trust, Identity	Confidentiality, Integrity, Availability, Accountability, Privacy

(continued)

Table 1. (*continued*)

Security Issues and Concerns	Major Compromised Security Attributes	Minor Compromised Security Attributes
Unidentified Risk Report and Service Level Agreement	Confidentiality, Deferment	Privacy, Trust, Compliance, Availability
Compliance Risks	Audit and Compliance	Accountability, Confidentiality, Integrity, Availability
Location Transparency	Trust, Privacy, Compliance	Availability, Integrity, Accountability
Insider Attacks/Wicked Insiders	Confidentiality, Privacy, Integrity, Trust, Concealment	Authentication, Accountability, Identity, Authorization
Accountability and Auditing	Accountability, Audit, Compliance	Confidentiality, Integrity, Availability, Privacy
Use of Proper Secure Protocols and Security Standards	Compliance, Audit, Identity, Trust	Confidentiality, Integrity, Availability, Privacy, Authentication, Authorization
Virtualization Risks	Reliability, Diligence	Availability, Confidentiality, Integrity
Secure Patches and Updates	Reliability, Diligence	Integrity, Availability, Confidentiality
Data Protection and Data Privacy	Privacy, Compliance, Confidentiality, Trust	NonRepudiation
Data Crash and Data Loss	Availability, System and Network Auditing, Privacy, Confidentiality	Integrity, Trust, Robustness
Data Interception	Confidentiality, Integrity, Auditability, Trust, Authentication	Availability, Authorization, Accountability
Proper use of Strong Cryptographic Functions	Privacy, Integrity, Confidentiality, Authentication, Authorization, Robustness, Non-Repudiation, Identity	Accountability, Trust
Insecure API	Complete Information Security and Data Privacy Failure	Complete Information Security and Data Privacy Failure
Account, Service, Traffic and Session/TCP Hijacking	Confidentiality, Trust, Authorization, Identity, Integrity, Authentication	Non-Repudiation, Accountability

(*continued*)

Table 1. (*continued*)

Security Issues and Concerns	Major Compromised Security Attributes	Minor Compromised Security Attributes
Web-Based Attacks	Availability, Trust, Authentication, Integrity, Authorization, Confidentiality, Privacy	Non-Repudiation, Accountability, Reliability
Privilege Escalation	Confidentiality, Trust, Authorization, Identity	Non-Repudiation, Accountability, Availability

4 Conclusion

The cloud environment is rapidly changing, and more changes will be witnessing in the coming years that lead to many risks, challenges, and security concerns. In light of this study, it can be tell that most prominent ones are the presence of unencrypted data in the cloud environment, possibility of data loss or data leakage, issues related to data privacy, regulatory compliances, unauthorized access to data, insecure configurations, or mis-configurations in services, insecure interfaces, use of proper secure protocols and security standards, misuse and iniquitous use of Cloud Computing Environment and proper handling and data movement in cloud environment. Cloud Service Providers are currently implementing containerization rather than virtualization to make the cloud environment more secure and decline the overabundance use or wastage of resources it occurred because of the utilization of virtualization. Cloud Service Providers are presently implementing Zero Trust User Access controls to minimize user risk along with device risk and they are also getting compliant to standards such as PCI DSS, ISO 27001, HIPAA, etc. Now, there also recently published standards such as ISO 27017 which provides information security controls for cloud services and ISO 27018 which focuses on protection of personal data (PII) on the cloud. This paper talked about every one of these viewpoints altogether in detail.

When organizations witness any cyber threat or cyberattack, most of the time they do not have any clarity about all the security attributes that can be compromised or have been compromised. So, the response takes a lot of time and sometimes it takes several months for an organization to realize that were compromised. This issue increases when security issues arises at once. The mapping of security issues with compromised security attribute shows that for every security issue and concern there are several security attributes that can be compromised. These attributes have both long-term and short-term impact, but the criticality of the issues and concerns is enhanced when any security attribute is un-noticed. It gives a clear picture about how the organizations should prepare and respond to security issues and concerns in a cloud environment.

References

1. NIST. https://nvlpubs.nist.gov/nistpubs/Legacy/SP/nistspecialpublication800-145.pdf
2. https://www.researchgate.net/publication/241195178/figure/fig2/AS:400869486022664
   @1472586141957/NIST-Visual-Model-of-Cloud-Computing-a-Service-Models-Cloud-com
   puting-can-be-classified.png
3. Surabhi, C.H., Gunalan, B.: A review of secure data sharing in cloud computing. Int. J.
   Comput. Trends Technol. **30**(3), 152–156 (2015)
4. https://www.darkreading.com/threat-intelligence/the-rising-tide-of-a-crimeware-as-a-ser
   vice/d/d-id/1329102
5. https://www.slideshare.net/InteropMumbai2009/sameer-ratolikar-crimeware-attacks-def
   enses-interop-mumbai-2009
6. Security Guidelines for Critical Areas of Focus in Cloud Computing, vol. 3. http://www.clo
   udsecurityalliance.org/guidance/csaguide.v3.0.pdf
7. Cloud Computing Benefits, Risks and Recommendations for Information Security.
   Rev. B (2012). https://resilience.enisa.europa.eu/cloud-security-and-resilience/publications/
   cloud-computing-benefits-risks-and-recommendations-for-information-security
8. Cloud Computing Benefits, Risks and Recommendations for Information Security Initial
   Release. Rev. A (November–December 2009). https://www.enisa.europa.eu/publications/
   cloud-computing-riskassessment/at_download/fullReport
9. Albugmi, A., Alassafi, M., Walters, R., Wills, G.: Data security in cloud computing. In:
   Proceedings of the 2016 Fifth International Conference on Future Generation Communication
   Technologies (FGCT), 17–19 Aug 2016, London, UK. IEEE (2016). https://doi.org/10.1109/
   FGCT.2016.7605062
10. Varsha, Wadhwa, A., Gupta, S.: Study of security issues in cloud computing. Int. J. Comp.
    Sci. Mob. Comput. **6**(4), 230–234 (2015)
11. Khan, N., Husain, M.S.: A survey on elasticity in cloud computing. In: Proceedings of the
    IEEE International Conference on Engineering and Technology (ICETECH), Coimbatore,
    Tamil Nadu, India (2015)
12. Singh, S., SikJeong, Y., Park, J.H.: A survey on cloud computing security: issues, threats, and
    solutions. J. Netw. Comput. Appl. **75**, 200–222 (2016)
13. Almorsy, M., Grundy, J., Müller, I.: An Analysis of the Cloud Computing Security Problem
14. Shah, H., Anandane, S.S.: Security Issues on Cloud Computing. arXiv:1308.5996 (2013)
15. Jamil, D., Zaki, H.: Security issues in cloud computing and countermeasures. Int. J. Eng. Sci.
    Technol. **3** (2011)
16. Chandrahasan, R.K., Priya, S.S., Arockiam, L.: Research challenges and security issues in
    cloud computing. Int. J. Comput. Intell. Inform. Secur., **3**(3) (2012)
17. https://en.wikipedia.org/wiki/California_Consumer_Privacy_Act
18. https://en.wikipedia.org/wiki/General_Data_Protection_Regulation
19. Kalaiprasath, R., Elankavir, R., Kumar, U.: Cloud security and compliance - a semantic
    approach in end to end security. Int. J. Mech. Eng. Technol. **8**(5), 987–994 (2017)
20. Kaura, W.C.N., Lal, A.: Survey paper on cloud computing security. In: 2017 International Con-
    ference on Innovations in Information, Embedded and Communication Systems (ICIIECS),
    Coimbatore, pp. 1–6 (2017). https://doi.org/10.1109/ICIIECS.2017.8276134
21. Dhamija, R., Dusseault, L.: The seven flaws of identity management: usability and security
    challenges. IEEE Secur. Privacy Mag. **6**(2), 24–29 (2008)
22. Ducatel, G.: Identity as a service- a cloud based common capability. In: IEEE Conference
    on Communications and Network Security (CNS), Florence, pp. 675–679 (2015). https://doi.
    org/10.1109/CNS.2015.7346886

23. Zhang, N., Liu, D., Zhang, Y.: A research on cloud computing security. In: International Conference on Information Technology and Applications, Chengdu, pp. 370–373 (2013). https://doi.org/10.1109/ITA.2013.91
24. Shariati, S.M., Abouzarjomehri, Ahmadzadegan, M.H.: Challenges and security issues in cloud computing from two perspectives: data security and privacy protection. In: 2nd International Conference on Knowledge-Based Engineering and Innovation (KBEI), Tehran, pp. 1078–1082 (2015). https://doi.org/10.1109/KBEI.2015.7436196
25. Irfan, M., Usman, M., Zhuang, Y., Fong, S.: A critical review of security threats in cloud computing. In: 3rd International Symposium on Computational and Business Intelligence (ISCBI), Bali, pp. 105–111 (2015). https://doi.org/10.1109/ISCBI.2015.26
26. Deshpande, P., Sharma, S.C., Kumar, P.S.: Security threats in cloud computing. In: International Conference on Computing, Communication & Automation, Noida, pp. 632–636 (2015). https://doi.org/10.1109/CCAA.2015.7148450
27. Tabrizchi, H., Kuchaki, Rafsanjani, M.: A survey on security challenges in cloud computing: issues, threats, and solutions. J. Supercomput. **76**(12), 9493–9532 (2020). https://doi.org/10.1007/s11227-020-03213-1
28. Kandias, M., Virvilis, N., Gritzalis, D.: The insider threat in cloud computing. In: Bologna, S., Hämmerli, B., Gritzalis, D., Wolthusen, S. (eds.) CRITIS 2011. LNCS, vol. 6983, pp. 93–103. Springer, Heidelberg (2013). https://doi.org/10.1007/978-3-642-41476-3_8
29. Chitturi, A.K., Swarnalatha, P.: Exploration of various cloud security challenges and threats. In: Das, K.N., Bansal, J.C., Deep, K., Nagar, A.K., Pathipooranam, P., Naidu, R.C. (eds.) Soft Computing for Problem Solving. AISC, vol. 1057, pp. 891–899. Springer, Singapore (2020). https://doi.org/10.1007/978-981-15-0184-5_76
30. Hashizume, K., Rosado, D.G., Fernández-Medina, E.: An analysis of security issues for cloud computing. J. Int. Serv. Appl. **4** (2013). https://doi.org/10.1186/1869-0238-4-55

Detection of Malicious Executable in Linux Environment Using Tree-Based Classifiers

Vaishali[1]($\boxtimes$) (iD), C. Rama Krishna[1] (iD), and Sanjay Sharma[2] (iD)

[1] National Institute of Technical Teachers Training and Research, Chandigarh, India
[2] Indian Institute of Technology, Kanpur, India
sanjlay.cse@nitttrchd.ac.in

Abstract. The exponential growth of the users' activities on the internet invites hackers to give birth to "Malware." Malware is a software which is specially designed to steal user's confidential data and damage network. Linux is a UNIX-based operating system and very popular in a while ago for several reasons (such as security features, open-source). In this paper, we present a Machine Learning based detection approach by using the hybrid analysis technique (static and dynamic) to detect unknown malware from the Linux operating system. Our proposed approach has been validating the malware detection using malware dataset from virus share and benign dataset from our college lab systems. We select the top 10 features by using Gain Ratio and Symmetric Uncertainty feature selection methods available in the WEKA. We used multiple classifiers such as Random Forest, J48, and REPTree. Out of these, J48 gave 99.82% detection accuracy with a 0.002% false-positive rate.

Keywords: Malware detection · Hybrid analysis · Linux operating system · WEKA · Machine Learning

1 Introduction

Malware is a software specially designed to infect a computer by executing malicious activities for getting user's essential data. Antivirus companies had proposed various solutions to detect known malware using a pattern matching technique (signature-based approach). However, modern malware is highly advanced and able to changes its appearance to bypass signature-based detection. Signature-based is insufficien"t for detecting advanced malware (polymorphic and metamorphic) [1]. In the literature, Linux malware detection methods hardly studied as compared to the windows operating system. The existing security systems cannot provide a complete solution for Linux OS from malware attacks [2, 4]. Nowadays, Attackers used the code obfuscation technique to develop a packed and encrypted version of malware using existing malware. This type of malware can hide in the user's system without being detected for an extended period of time. Currently, malware analysts working with two approaches for analyses called static and dynamic analysis.

© Springer Nature Switzerland AG 2021
R. Agrawal et al. (Eds.): ICCEDE 2020, CCIS 1436, pp. 41–50, 2021.
https://doi.org/10.1007/978-3-030-84842-2_3

In static analysis, the file is analyzed by studying the structure and data present in it. It is fast and easy to deploy because this process performs without executing the file. But there are some limitations – it fails to detect the packed and encrypted malware [3]. This limitation motivates us to work with secondary analysis, i.e., dynamic analysis. It examines its running state of the malware program in a secure environment (sandbox). It can detect packed and encrypted malware. It has limitations, too, it only finds defects in the executed part of the code, and some malware hides their exact behavior when running in a controlled environment [5].

Both analyses have their advantages and disadvantages. Therefore the combination of both the analysis utilizes the features of each other, and it may improve the accuracy of the malware detection.

In this paper, we perform a combination of both analyses. We first analyze the internal structure of the -ELF file format (used by the Linux OS). Second, we run the executable in LIMON sandbox for 12 s to trace the system calls and commands used by the system to perform any task. This analysis helps us classify the set of features that can use to segregate malware executable from benign executable. After that, we apply the pre-processing filters to remove the unneeded features from our feature set. Finally, we are remaining with the features used as input to the selected classifiers. Our Experimental results show that the presented approach classified the malware executable with 99.82% accuracy.

To summarize, the contributions of this paper are as follows:

- We propose the hybrid analysis technique that allows us to inspect the executable before and after executing the file by performing the static and dynamic analysis. Static analysis helps us to observe the behavior of the executable without implementing it into the system. The dynamic analysis helps us find the defects in code by observing the executable runtime behavior in a controlled environment. This approach helps us to detect unknown malware.
- We developed a system that analyzes Linux operating system executable by executing them in a virtual machine environment (LIMON Sandbox). Further, we disassemble the files (using reverse engineering tool) to extract the file info without executing it.
- We evaluated the proposed system using a large number of malware samples and demonstrate that we were able to identify the behavior that may not be achievable by performing basic analysis individually.

The Rest of the paper is organized as follows: In Sect. 2, we discussed the related work, discussion about static and dynamic analysis in Sect. 3 and Sect. 4 presents the proposed methodology. In Sect. 5 discuss the experiment and results. Finally, Sect. 6 concludes the paper with future directions.

2   Related Work

M. G. Schultz et al. [6] proposed the machine learning-based technique to detect malicious files in the Windows operating system using static analysis. They used PE, byte n-gram, and strings for extracting the features. Classification algorithms used by the authors: Naïve Bayes, Ripple Learning Rules, Multi-Naïve Bayes, and J. Z. Kolter et al. [7] proposed a system by using data mining and machine learning technique to classify the malware-infected file in the wild. N-gram was used as a feature to extract the byte sequence from executable. For further classification, they used SVM (Support Vector Machine), Boosted SVM, IBK (Instance-Based Learner), Naïve Bayes, Boosted Naïve Bayes, Decision Tree, Boosted Decision tree. FarrukhShahzad et al. [8] used the ELF (Executable and Linkable Format) executable to statically analyzing the malware on the Linux platform. The total dataset they used was 709. They used the ELF header for extracting features. For selecting features, they have used Info Gain method. The author used four machine learning algorithms i.e., C4.5 Rules, Ripper, PART, and J48 decision tree. FarrukhShahzad et al. [9] introduced genetic footprint concept to detect the essential information extracted from the kernel process control blocks to find malicious files while in execution. S. M. JinrongBai et al. [10] proposed a technique to find malicious executable from the Linux operating system by extracting system calls from the ELF symbol table as a feature. The authors used 1519 files for presenting their work. Asmitha KA et al. [11] proposed an approach in which they detected the malicious executable from the Linux operating system by using dynamic analysis. The authors used 668 files for the experiment. They used system calls as a feature extracted by using "strace" tool to observe the behavior of the processes during run time. For the classification they used: IBK-5, Naïve Bayes,Random Forest, Ada boost M1 (J48): all available in WEKA machine learning-based GUI tool. Asmitha K A et al. [12] implemented an approach based upon correlation to classify the malicious and benign executable. A total of 668 files were used for the implementation. To implement this approach, they particularly focused on the system calls and used probabilistic information gain method for selecting promising features. They usedJ48, Ada boost, and Random Forest for the classification.

- Existing work on malware detection used either static analysis or dynamic analysis.
- As we studied in our literature survey, authors used a very small dataset that is not sufficient to perform the task using machine learning.

3 Methodology

In this part, we describe the flow diagram of our methodology. Figure 1 shows the proposed methodology. It contains a dataset, feature selection module, and classification module. All of them explained in the next sections.

3.1 Building Dataset

We have collected 24000 files in which out of 24000 files, 12000 are benign, and 12000 are malware files. Malware sample collected from virusshare [13] and the benign samples collected from /bin, /sbin, /usr/bin Linux directories. During the literature survey, we found that dataset plays a vital role in machine learning technique i.e.

- For most of the "average" problems, we should have 10,000 to 100,000 examples. So we have collected 24000 files [14].

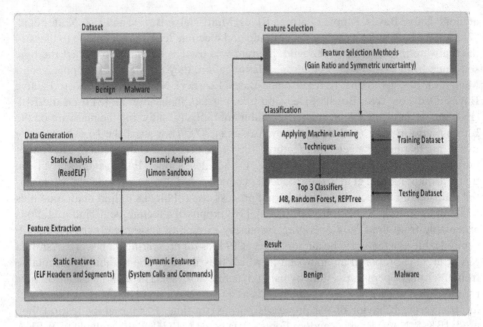

Fig. 1. Flow Diagram of Methodology

- It is good to collect malware samples from different families (Forex Virus, Worm, Trojan, Backdoor). Our dataset has collected malware samples from almost eight families i.e., Virus, Worm, Trojan, Botnet, Rootkit, Adware, Ransomware, and Backdoor.
- In our approach, we are using static analysis also. In this approach, we disassemble executable using readelf utility present in the Linux operating system. Thus, we have collected benign files from both 32-bit and 64-bit machines.

For the training and testing of our selected classifiers, we used ten-fold cross-validation [15].

3.2 Feature Extraction

Feature extraction is a vital step in designing a model. This process performed to reduce the over fitting issue and improve data visualization.

Static Analysis and Static Features: For static analysis, features extracted from the elf header and the segments. In the elf file, "Header" holds useful information like the type of elf, architecture, elf version, and other essential information required. The segments contain information that is necessary during the run time of the file [16]. For analysis, we used the readelf utility [14] on our dataset to extract useful features. Readelf is a utility that comes under the gnu binary utilities displays the information about one and more elf format object files. Figure 2 shows the frequency of the features present in both benign and malware executable. Elf header and segment extracted features are sorts according to the frequency of occurrences within the files.

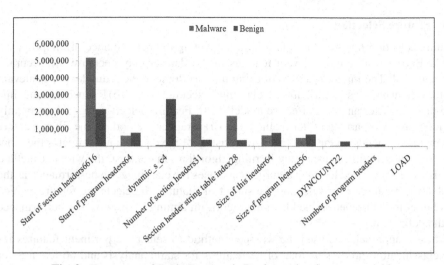

Fig. 2. Frequency of Static Features in Benign and malware executable

Dynamic Analysis and Dynamic Features: Analysis performed by extracting features from system calls and command used by executable during execution time. System calls are instructions given by the os to use hardware at a low-level for executing the program. For this purpose, the limon sandbox [17] installed on ubuntu 18.04. It used to analyze and run the malware files, and after that, it generates an analysis result of the malware behavior at the time of execution. Figure 3 shows the frequency of the dynamic features present in both malware and benign.

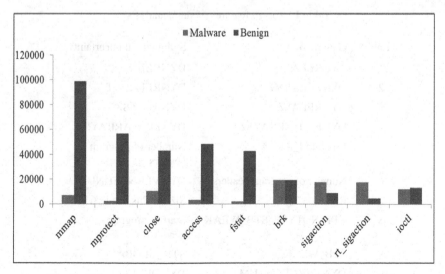

Fig. 3. Frequency of dynamic features in benign and malware executable

3.3 Feature Selection

Feature selection plays a manifold role in improving the performance of the proposed work. Because of some irrelevant features in the dataset may decrease the accuracy of the model. The main objectives of using this (a) Remove the redundant or irrelevant features (that have less contribution in classifier's accuracy rate), (b) Reduce training time and provide faster and cost-effective models [18]. Feature Selection algorithms mainly divided into two parts: (i) filter method and (ii) wrapper method. In the filter method, the method depends on the general characteristics of the dataset and evaluates the input features' subset without using any learning algorithm. In contrast, the wrapper method needs a predetermined learning algorithm and uses the classification performance as the evaluation parameter for selecting the subset of features. It selects the features which suit better to the predetermined learning algorithm aiming to improve the performance of the defined model.

In our approach, we used the wrapper method to select the pertinent features for the classification process. A total of 82 features for static analysis and 66 features for dynamic analysis are extracted. However, most of the features are not useful and redundant. Therefore, we used two feature selection techniques: Gain Ratio and Symmetric Uncertainty to improve accuracy and resolve over fitting issues for our proposed approach. By using the Gain ratio and symmetrical uncertainty method –with static analysis, we are remaining with 72 and 65 features, respectively. Using the same selection methods –with dynamic analysis, we are remaining with 14 (Gain ratio) and 12 (symmetrical uncertainty) features.

The proposed approach selected top 10 features as described in Table 1 Gain ratio and symmetrical uncertainty feature selection method is working with the Rank method. So the ranking of the selected features is done with the help of these ranking methods.

Table 1. Top 10 features of static analysis

Rank	Gain ratio	Symmetrical uncertainty
1	DYNRELA	DYNRELA
2	DYNRELAENT	DYNRELAENT
3	DYNRELASZ	DYNRELASZ
4	DYNFINI_ARRAYSZ	DYNFINI_ARRAYSZ
5	DYNFINI_ARRAY	Number of program headers
6	Number of program headers	DYNVERNEEDNUM
7	RELA	Size of this header64
8	STT_NOTYPE_STB_WEAK	Start of program headers64
9	STB_WEAK	STB_GLOBAL
10	DYNVERNEEDNUM	DYNDEBUG

Table 2. Top 10 features of dynamic analysis

Rank	Gain ratio	Symmetrical uncertainty
1	Access	Access
2	Fstat	Fstat
3	Mmap	Mmap
4	Brk	Brk
5	Mprotect	Mprotect
6	Fork	Fork
7	Munmap	Close
8	wait4	Ioctl
9	Getpid	rt_sigaction
10	Write	Sigaction

After selecting these top 10 features for static and dynamic analysis, we merge them to perform the hybrid analysis. In Tables 3 and 4 shows the comparison of static and hybrid analysis results.

3.4 Training of the Classifiers

The next step is to train the model for selecting the best classifier based on accuracy for detecting malware. To perform this task, we compare the performance of different classifiers using the top 10 features shown in Tables 1 and 2. We examined 3 tree-based classifiers: Decision Tree (J48), Random Forest, and Fast Decision Tree Learner (REP-Tree) available in WEKA. In the case of accuracy, the decision tree improves better with the increasing data. With the more diverse and large data, it could generate more accurate empirically [19]. An open-source tool WEKA can be accessed by GUI, standard terminal application, or through Java API [20]. We enforce the selected classifiers on feature selection methods using 10-fold cross-validation to train our classifiers. The K-fold cross-validation process used to check the skills of the machine learning model. Tables 3 and 4 show each selected classifier's accuracy with two feature selection methods (Gain Ratio and Symmetric Uncertainty).

In Table 3, the static analysis performed with the gain ratio method gives us the best result compared to the symmetric uncertainty, and we got 99.33% accuracy in the case of Random forest. With the same feature selection method, the hybrid analysis (Table 4) gave 99.82% accuracy with the J48 classifier. So in our proposed work, the hybrid analysis performed better than the static analysis for detecting malicious files in Linux OS.

4   Results and Discussion

As discussed in our above sections, we collected our malware dataset from virus share and benign dataset from Linux directories. We performed dynamic and static analysis as a different task and merged both analysis results to perform the hybrid analysis. For the static analysis, we extracted features from ELF header and segments. For dynamic analysis, we extracted the features from system calls and commands. Next, to remove the irrelevant features from the dataset, we used two Feature Selection method. We found the top 10 features that enforced on classification process done by using three tree-based classifiers (J48, Random Forest, and REPTree). Evaluation of the top three classifiers is done in WEKA to find how efficiently they work to find the unknown malware. An evaluation performed by using TPR (True Positive Rate), TNR (True Negative Rate), FPR (False Positive Rate), and FNR (False Negative Rate). Accuracy calculated using Eq. 1.

$$\text{Accuracy} = \frac{correctlyPredictedvalues}{outofalltheclasses} \qquad (1)$$

Table 3. Static analysis results using gain ratio method

Class	J48			Random forest			REPTreee		
	TPR	FPR	Accuracy	TPR	FPR	Accuracy	TPR	FPR	Accuracy
Benign	0.986	0.000	99.30%	0.987	0.000		0.986	0.000	99.31%
Malware	1.00	0.014		1.00	0.013	99.33%	1.00	0.014	
Avg. Weight	0.993	0.007		0.993	0.007		0.993	0.007	

Table 4. Hybrid analysis results using gain ratio

Class	J48			Random forest			REPTreee		
	TPR	FPR	Accuracy	TPR	FPR	Accuracy	TPR	FPR	Accuracy
Benign	0.997	0.000	99.82%	0.991	0.000	99.54%	0.995	0.001	99.67%
Malware	1.00	0.003		1.00	0.009		0.99	0.005	
Avg. Weight	0.998	0.002		0.995	0.005		0.997	0.003	

Tables 3 and 4 show our results on static analysis features and hybrid analysis features, respectively. As we can see in Table 3, we used three tree-based classifiers (J48, Random Forest, and REPTree). We got the best detection accuracy with the Random Forest classifier with .007 FPR (False Positive Rate). In Table 4, we used the same dataset and merged the static and dynamic analysis features and applied it to the same tree-based classifiers. We got better detection accuracy with the J48 classifier with .002 FPR (False Positive Rate). Our proposed approach aims to achieve high TPR (True Positive Rate) for the malicious file in which malicious executable detection rate is high.

In Table 5, we compare our work with previously published work. We used a combination of two analysis to detect advanced malware e.g., Encrypted, Packed, Anti- VM.

This type of malware is unable to detect by implementing static and dynamic analysis individually.

Table 5. Comparisons with previous published work

Sno	Authors Name	Dataset	Types of Analysis	Types of Features	Accuracy
1	F.Shahzad, M.Farooq [7]	709 B 709 M	Static Analysis	ELF Structure	99%
2	S.M., JinrongBai, Y.Yang, Y.MA [9]	756 B 763 M	Static Analysis	Symbol table	98%
3	F.Shahzad, M.Shahzad, M.Farooq [8]	105 B 114 M	Dynamic Analysis	Process control block	96%
4	K.A.Asmitha, P.Vinod [10]	442 B 226 M	Dynamic Analysis	System calls	99.4%
5	Our Work	12000 B 12000 M	Static and Dynamic Analysis	ELF Header, Segments, System calls & commands	99.82%

5 Conclusions

Malware is a software specially designed to infect a computer by executing malicious activities for getting user's essential data. We proposed a Machine Learning based detection approach by using a hybrid analysis technique (static and dynamic) to detect unknown malware from the Linux operating system. Our proposed approach has been validated using malware dataset from virusshare and benign dataset from our college lab systems. The proposed system results show that detection accuracy increased by employing the hybrid analysis technique (static and dynamic). We integrated features of both the analysis (static and dynamic) to improve detection accuracy (99.82%). In the future, we will work on different file formats and choose fewer features to minimize the system's overall complexity.

References

1. WatchGuard Network Security Solution Company. https://www.watchguard.com/. Accessed 5 Jan 2020
2. Cozzi, E., Graziano, M., Fratantonio, Y., Balzarotti, D.: Understanding linux malware. In: IEEE Symposium on Security and Privacy (SP), San Francisco, CA, pp. 161–175 (2018). https://doi.org/10.1109/SP.2018.00054

3. Sharma, S., Rama Krishna, C., Sahay, S.K.: Detection of advanced malware by machine learning techniques. In: Ray, K., Sharma, T.K., Rawat, S., Saini, R.K., Bandyopadhyay, A. (eds.) Soft Computing: Theories and Applications. AISC, vol. 742, pp. 333–342. Springer, Singapore (2019). https://doi.org/10.1007/978-981-13-0589-4_31
4. Yaswinski, M.R., Chowdhury, M.M., Jochen, M.: Linux security: a survey. In: IEEE International Conference on Electro Information Technology (EIT), Brookings, SD, USA, pp. 357–362 (2019). https://doi.org/10.1109/EIT.2019.8834112
5. https://www.cyberbit.com/blog/endpoint-security/anti-vm-and-anti-sandbox-explained/. Accessed 9 Jan 2020
6. Schultz, M.G., Eskin, E., Zadok, F., Stolfo, S.J.: Data mining methods for detection of new malicious executables. In: IEEE Symposium on Security and Privacy (S&P), Oakland, CA, USA, pp. 38–49 (2001). https://doi.org/10.1109/SECPRI.2001.924286
7. Kolter, J.Z., Maloof, M.A.: Learning to detect and classify malicious executables in the wild. In: 10th ACM SIGInternational Conference on Knowledge Discovery and Data Mining (KDD), vol. 7, pp. 2721–2744 (2004). https://doi.org/10.1145/1014052
8. Shahzad, F., Farooq, M.: ELF-miner: using structural knowledge and data mining methods to detect new (linux) malicious executables. Knowl. Inf. Syst. 30(3), 589–612 (2011). https://doi.org/10.1007/s10115-011-0393-5
9. Shahzad, F., Shahzad, M., Farooq, M.: In-execution dynamic malware analysis and detection by mining information in process control blocks of linux OS. Inf. Sci. 231, 45–63 (2013). https://doi.org/10.1016/j.ins.2011.09.016
10. JinrongBai, S.M., Yang, Y., MA, Y.: Malware detection through mining symbol table of linux executables. Info. Technol. J. 12, 380–384 (2012). https://doi.org/10.3923/itj.2013.380.384
11. Asmitha, K.A., Vinod, P.: A machine learning approach for linux malware detection. In: International Conference on Issues and Challenges in Intelligent Computing Techniques (ICICT), Ghaziabad, pp. 825–830. IEEE (2014). https://doi.org/10.1109/ICICICT.2014.6781387
12. Asmitha, K.A., Vinod, P.: Linux malware detection using extended–symmetric uncertainty. In: Chakraborty, R.S., Matyas, V., Schaumont, P. (eds.) SPACE 2014. LNCS, vol. 8804, pp. 319–332. Springer, Cham (2014). https://doi.org/10.1007/978-3-319-12060-7_21
13. Virusshare. https://virusshare.com/. Accessed 8 Jan 2020
14. https://ftp.gnu.org/old-gnu/Manuals/binutils-2.12/html_node/binutils_16.html. Accessed 9 Jan 2020
15. A Gentle Introduction to k-fold Cross-Validation. https://machinelearningmastery.com/k-fold-cross-validation/. Accessed 8 Jan 2020
16. Executable and Linkable Format (ELF). https://www.cs.cmu.edu/. Accessed 2020
17. Monnappa22/Limon. https://github.com/monnappa22/Limon/blob/master/Setting_up_and_configuring_Limon.pdf. Accessed 8 Jan 2020
18. Ali, S.I., Shahzad, W.: A feature subset selection method based on symmetric uncertainty and ant colony optimization. In: International Conference on Emerging Technologies, Islamabad, pp. 1–6. IEEE (2012). https://doi.org/10.1109/ICET.2012.6375420
19. Hyontai, S.: Performance of machine learning algorithms and diversity in data. In: MATEC Web of Conference, vol. 210, pp. 04019 (2018). https://doi.org/10.1051/matecconf/201821004019
20. WEKA3. https://www.cs.waikato.ac.nz/ml/weka/. Accessed 8 Jan 2020

Evading Detection Systems by Generating Adversarial Malware Examples

Suyash Gupta[✉], Sahil Lamba, Nipun Soni, and Prakhar Priyadarshi

Information Technology, Bharati Vidyapeeth's College of Engineering, New Delhi, India
{nipunsoni.it1,Priyadarshi.prakhar}@bvp.edu.in

Abstract. Machine Learning is an immensely valuable tool nto ensure advanced identification and safety mechanisms for protecting our personal information when it comes to cyber security. The Generative Adversarial Network (GAN), which is the main focus of this article, is a particularly strong machine learning principle. The GAN has numerous information defense uses, including the validation of current threats outside the traditional monitoring system. As GANs become more popular, the need to defend against and recognize GAN attacks is also becoming increasingly urgent. This paper proposes a Genetic Alteration Network (GAN) model called Mal-wareGAN to generate malware examples of adversaries that can bypass model detection based on black box learning. Malware-GAN uses a replacement detector to match the black-box malwset device. A generative network model was trained to minimize the malicious probabilities of the replacement detector in adverse instances. Malware-GAN's advantage over conventional gradient-dependent adversarial examples is that Malware-GAN can reduce the detection rate to almost zero and make it difficult to work defensively against adverse examples.

Keywords: Black box attack · Neural network replacement · Probability distribution · Benign program · Malware detection

1 Introduction

GANs are one of artificial intelligence's newest ideas, utilizing cutting-edge technology. Let's look at the word's definition: adversarial. In its initial application in AI, this term refers to an example type designed to deceive an evaluating neural net or another machine-learning model. As the usage of machine learning in security applications has grown, this example has become increasingly essential. The current state of the art focuses on photos, but it could be applied to other file formats in the future. In theory, these matting systems may be even more vulnerable because only a slight change in an image must be made in order to ensure that it remains recognizable to humans. Other formats would seem the same while additional material is available at the end. This leads to various (and defensive) attacks.

© Springer Nature Switzerland AG 2021
R. Agrawal et al. (Eds.): ICCEDE 2020, CCIS 1436, pp. 51–60, 2021.
https://doi.org/10.1007/978-3-030-84842-2_4

Generative adversarial networks, according to O'Reilly media [1] are "neural networks that learn how to produce synthetic data comparable to some known input data." The above-mentioned' antagonistic' has a slightly different meaning than these networks. In this example, the phrase refers to two neural networks that compete to make a game happen: a generator and a discriminator. The goal of the game is to fool the generator by using instances that are similar to those in the training set [2]. This hypothesis was first proposed in a study [6].

When the discriminator rejects the case supplied by the generator, the generator will learn a little more about how a good example looks. Keep in mind that the generator must start with a probability distribution. Sometimes it's just the standard distribution that makes the GAN so adaptable and simple to set up. You can choose a better probability distribution if you know more about the real cases. The discriminator usually functions as a binary distinction, i.e. it states' yes' to an example or' no.' It simplifies the design and makes it realistic for GANs to choose only two options to allow the discriminator [7].

Why can you use real examples to approach the generator? Whenever the discriminator tries, it sends the power generator a signal to tell them what a real example it looks like. Technically, this is the difference gradient, so that you can see that as a measure of closeness/quality and directions. In other words, data on the proximity and approach of the generator leaks from the discriminator. The generator gene ideally erases examples so well as examples that distinguish between real and generated examples.

The use of GAN in information security is not just the generation of data, but even the detection mechanisms can be avoided [15]. This can be applied to malware development, which bypasses the detection systems of machine learning. The paper Generating Adversarial Malware Examples of GAN-based Black-Box Attacks [3] is deeply covered in this topic.

This work discusses another GAN program, Malware-GAN, which can produce such malware and is even better than other adversary learning methods. This attack is effective as it is done by black box schemes, so that the attacker does not know the method of detection. You can see the basic architecture of Malware-GAN in the figure below. The concept is like a standard GAN except that the Black-Box detector is used as a discriminator and a mixture of noise and malware is applied to the generator [9].

The discriminator often receives strong examples to further educate the generator about what is labeled "not malware there are also widespread uses of this technique. This means that attackers need to learn less about the device in the process to effectively target it by offering a new approach to bypass Blackbox malware detection [12].Using a machine to learn how to build malware ensures that this malware can have even greater subtleties and complexity. It is important to note that when using a machine-based learning detection method, they will have their respective bugs.

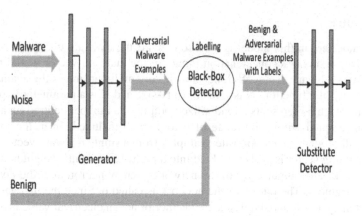

Fig. 1. Architecture of Malware-GAN

2 Architecture of Malware-GAN

2.1 Overview

The architecture of Malware-GAN is illustrated in Fig. 1. The black box detector is a third party device which uses malware detection algorithms based on the learning machine. We think that malware authors know what kind of black box detector features they use. Malware authors do not have access to qualified model parameters, they do not know the algorithm used to learn the machine. In order to identify their programmers, malware writers may receive results from a blackbox sensor [11]. The entire model has both neural power grids, a generator and a replacement detector. A black box malware detector based on a learning system will be attacked by the generator and the replacement detector.

This paper only generates binary-characteristic opponents, provided that binary-characteristics are commonly used by researchers for malware detection and result in high detection accuracy. Here is an example of how to represent a program using the API function. When the M-APIs are used as functions, the program builds an M- dimensional function vector. The value of the d-th function is set to 1 for the program to call the d-th API, otherwise it will be fixed to 0 [13].

The main difference between this rule-set and existing algorithms is that the opposite examples are dynamically generated based on blackbox-detector feedback, whereas most of the current algorithms are based on static gradient approaches for constructing adverse examples.

The weights of the generator depend upon the distribution of the likelihood of adverse events from MalGAN. The data examples in the training sets and test set should adopt the same distributed probability or equivalent probability distributed in order to maximize the efficiency of the machine learning algorithm [17].Although the generator can adapt the distribution of the probability of negative examples to differentiate between the probability distribution of the blackbox detector training package. The generator is more likely to malclassify the malware as the black box detector in this case.

2.2 Generator

This generator here in this model is used to convert the malware characteristic vector in an adverse version. As concatenation input are the malware vector w and the noise vector N. W is a binary vector W-dimensional. Any m dimension is the availability or non-availability of a function. N is a vector in N-size and N is a parameter hyper.

The dimension n represents a randomized output of a number centred on a uniform distribution sampled within the range of 0 to 1, both included. In n, the mentioned generator will produce many opposite examples from a single malware vector.

The incoming vector is broken and fed into a multi-layer, multi-weight neural introducing network. The output layer of the network is an W-neuron, and the layer of the last layer is sigmoid. The output of the network is called o. Since the malware feature values are binary, o is binarized based on whether or not an electrical value is more than 0.5 and produces an binary vector o^3.

We expect to incorporate some unnecessary malware features while creating negative examples of biological malware functions. This is hackable by removing a malware feature. For example, when the "WriteFile" API has been removed from software and malware crashes, the software will not perform normal writing functions. The elements not zero in the o^3 binary vector do not matter for the original malware.

In $w^3 = wo^3$, where a binary OR elementary operation is performed, the opposite example is finalised. w is a binary vector and thus gradients from the alternating detector to the generator cannot be repropagated. The smooth tt function will be defined to get the detector information in Formula 1.

$$tt_{\theta_g}(w, n) = \max(w, o) \tag{1}$$

m·a·x(,) is the max-operation element. If an element of w has value 1, tt is equally 1 and cannot transport the differentials backwards. If an element of w has a value of 0, tt's result is the actual number output of the neural network in the correct dimension, and gradient data can be passed through. It can be seen that w^3 will actually be the binarised transformation version of $tt_\theta(w, n)$.

2.3 Substitute Detector

As malicious-ware writers don't understand the blackbox detector's comprehensive structure, replacement detector correlates with the black box detector and offers details about the gradient training [19]. The in absence detector is a multiple layer neural weight introduction network that uses input as an x vector. The software is designated as nice and malware. We notice the estimated likelihood of x being malicious ware as D versus x.

A replacement detector's practice data consists of opponents of an example of a malware generator and benign programs obtained from more benevolent data collection by malicious authors. The basic truth marks of the training data are not included in the test of the alternative detector [22]. The object of the substitute detector is to fit the blackbox detector. First the black box detector detects this, and then it shows whether or not the software is benign or malicious ware. The substitute detector uses predicted tor labels in the blackbox.

2.4 Training Malware-GAN

In order to train malware writers, a malicious ware's set of data and a benign set of data should be collected first. Formula 2 determines the failure working of a replacement detector.

$$L_D = -E_{x \in BBBenign} \log(1 - D_{\theta d}(x)) \hspace{2cm} (2)$$

$$-E_{x \in BBMalware} \log D_{\theta d}(x) \hspace{2cm} (3)$$

The BB_{Benign} is a sequence of black-box-detector functions that are classified as harmless, and $BB_{Malware}$ is the group of programs that the black box-detector detects as malware.

LD should be reduced in favor of the weights of a replacement detector in order to train a replacement detector.

SBenign is the actual malicious ware set of data, not the black box detector malware package. The weights of the generator are reduced for LG [20].

By lowering LG, the malware's anticipated harmful likelihood is reduced, and the replacement detector is forced to accept it as benign. As the replacement detector tries to fit inside the black box, the generator preparation will fool the black box detector further.

Algorithm 1 demonstrates the entire training cycle of **Malware-GAN.**

Algorithm 1 The Process Training of algorithm

1: **while** not funneling **do**
2: Sample the mini-batch of malwares M
3: Generate GAN samples M' from the sample generator for M
4: Sample the mini-batch of harmless programs B
5: Label M' and B using the black-box detector
6: Update the substitute detector's weights θ_d/by descending along the gradient ∇
$\theta_d L_D$
7: Update the generator's weights θg by descending along the gradien∇t θg LG
  8: **end while**
In line 2 and line 4, different sizes of mini batches are used for malware and benign programs. The ratio of M
's size to B's size is the same as the ratio of the malware dataset's size to the benign dataset's size.

Fig. 2. Algorithm 1 demonstrates the entire training cycle of **Malware-GAN.**

3 Implementation

3.1 Comparison with the Gradient Based Algorithm to Generate Adversarial Examples

The current methods for creating negative examples are primarily for photos. The distinction between image and harmful functions is that image functions are continuous, whereas malware functions are binary [6]. They did not treat the malicious ware detection method as a black-box approach and claimed that malware developers had direct access to the neural network-dependent malware detection model architecture and weight. The error rate of the opposing examples ranges from 40% to 84% for particular hyperparameters. This gradient-based approach is not capable of producing zero TPR opponents, while the Malware-GAN produces a near null TPR with higher black-box assumptions.

They use the same algorithm to build an iterative strategy for malware opponents. The algorithm is most likely to change the malware mark for every iteration from malicious to benign. The algorithm modifies one function in each iteration until the malware has been detected as a benign program or until no functions can be changed. This algorithm was attempted to migrate to target a black box random forest recognition algorithm. A neural replacement network is designed to fit into a random black box. Adverse malware examples are generated based on neural network replacement gradient knowledge [8].

Figure 4 shows TPR for opposite examples in the iterative cycle. Remember that not all malicious ware samples have been modified for each iteration. If a malicious ware example has been recognized as a harmless program in earlier versions or none are the modifiable functions, the malware sample does not do anything on the algorithm at 93.52% and 90.96% respectively. In this case, most adversarial examples are identified in the black box by the random forest. The neural replacement network is trained on the original training set, although the probability distribution of adverse events varies significantly from the probability distribution of the initial training set after multiple iterations. Thus, the random black-box forest cannot be well approached by opposing instances with the neural replacement network. In this case, the adverse neural network replacement examples cannot fool the random black box forest. We tried to retrain the opponent's neural replacement network to better match the black-box random forest to the opposing instances [15] Existing examples of opponents of the full training set are used to retrain the neural network replacement function in each iteration.

As shown in Fig. 3, TPRs converge at 46.18% in training settings, which means that approximately half of the adverse events can still be found in the random forest black box. Therefore, the retrained model cannot generalize to the test set, except that the TPR is 90.12% on the test set. The unusual distribution of the probability of these adverse events limits the potential for generalization of the neural replacement network.

To change the original samples into opposing samples, Malware-GAN employs a generation network. Malware-GAN generates nearly no TPR on both the training and test sets thanks to the neural network's ability to represent complicated transformations in sufficient depth. Although the gradient-based approach's capacity to reflect is insufficient to produce high-quality unfavourable events.

3.2 Experimental Results

First we examine where Malware-GAN is using the same collection of training as the black box sensor. The true positive rate (TPR), in the case of malware detection, implies the malware detection rate. The decline in TPR will indicate how many malware samples bypass the detection algorithm successfully after an opponent attack. In Table 1, we present TPR on the training set and test set of initial samples and opponent examples.

For random forests and decision-taking bodies, both preparation and research range TPRs on opponent examples between 0.16% and 0.20% while TPRs on the initial samples

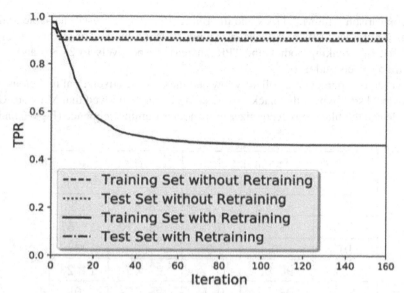

Fig. 3. The TPR on the opposite instances of the iterative method by using the Grosse algorithm.

surpass 93%. When the black box detector other classificators are used, Malware-GAN will the TPR to zero for the training and tests set on generated adversarial examples. That is, the blackbox detector is difficult to detect any malware created by the generator for all backend classifiers. This model has succeeded in completely avoiding such malware detection algorithms based on learning machines [14].

The logistic regression architectures and the assisted vector ma-Chinese are very close to neural networks. The replacement detector will therefore suit them with a high precision. For those classifiers, Malware-GAN can there- fore achieve zero TPR. While random wood and decision-making trees have very different structures than neural networks, Malware-GAN leads to non-zero TPRs. Random forest TPRs and decision trees are still quite small, so that the neural network is capable of representing other models with very different structures. The vote on the algorithms also produces zero TPR. We may infer that during the vote the classificators of identical structures are the majority of neural networks.

Figure 2 shows the TPR convergence curve for the training set and the validation set during the Malware-GAN training phase. The detector used in this case is random forest, since Table 1 is an extremely good random for est.

Near the 40th century, TPR converges to zero, but the convergence curve is a little moving, not a stream. This curve represents the normal un-stable training of GAN [19].

When Malware-GAN and the blackbox detector are taught on different training courses, the results will be reviewed. The new sensor will have a harder time matching the black-box detector trained on a new dataset. The experimental findings are shown in Table 2

TPR has a zero amount for SVM, MLP and VOTE, and LR's TPR is almost null. The findings are very close to Table 1.

In comparison with Mal, GAN and the Black- Box detector used the same training data, random forest TPRs and decision-making trees are higher for adverse example. Among decision-making bodies, the TPRs increase respectively to 2.18% and 2.11% for the training sets and tests.

However, two percent are still very low and most of the adversarial malicious ware entities would still bypass the black-box detector. It can be derived that Malware-GAN can yet delude the black box recognizer into another training sequence (Figs. 5 and 6).

	Training Set		Test Set	
	Original	Adver.	Original	Adver.
RF	98. 32	2. 73	98. 87	3. 56
LR	98. 53	10. 32	99. 27	11. 67
DT	0	0	100	0
SVM	98. 08	17. 36	97. 44	14. 23
MLP	98. 08	0. 71	98. 17	0
VOTE	98. 72	12. 13	96. 71	13. 51

Fig. 4. True positive rate of initial samples (in percentage) and negative entities when Malware-GAN and the black-box detector are trained in the same training package. —Adver.‖ represents adversarial examples.

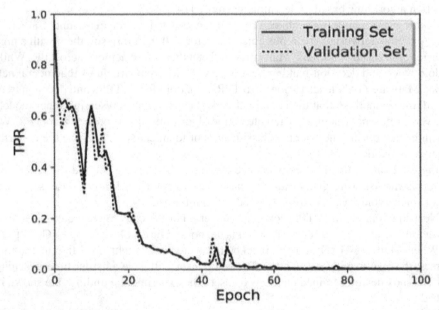

Fig. 5. Change of the true positive rate for the training set and time defined validation. The blackbox detector here is Random Wood. The vertical axis is the real positive scale, while the horizontal axis is epochal.

	Training Set		Test Set	
	Original	Adver.	Original	Adver.
RF	96. 88	4. 64	95. 27	7. 93
LR	94. 07	12. 53	96. 84	15. 24
DT	0	0	100	0
SVM	98. 17	18. 84	96. 71	14. 26
MLP	97. 98	1. 52	97. 81	0. 63
VOTE	98. 35	13. 81	98. 9	14. 15

Fig. 6. Real positive (in percentage) results and opposite instances when MalGAN and black box sensors on different training sets are trained. Adver represents adversarial example.

4 Conclusion

This paper suggested a new Malware-GAN algorithm to produce bad samples of a learning technology-based malicious ware detector in a blackbox. The black-box detector is fitted with a neural network replacement detector. The generator is designed to generate examples of the adversary which the replacement detector might trick. Experimental findings suggest that the black box detector is efficiently passed through the examples of the adversary.

The weight of the generator depends on the distribution of probability in opposite instances. Malware writers also can change the probability distribution by retraining MalGAN, thereby preventing them from up-to-date blackbox detectors and learning from them coherent patterns. Upgraded a black-box detector will disable malware writers. This way, a computer can difficultly learn algorithms based on malware.

References

1. Arjovsky, M., Bottou, L.: Towards principled methods for training generative adversarial networks. In: NIPS 2016 Workshop on Adversarial Training. In review for ICLR (2017)
2. Chen, X., Li, B., Vorobeychik, Y.: Evaluation of defensive methods for DNNS against multiple adversarial evasion models (2016)
3. Denton, E.L., Chintala, S., Fergus, R., et al.: Deep generative image models using a Laplacian pyramid of adversarial networks. In: Advances in Neural Information Processing Systems, pp. 1486–1494 (2015)
4. Goodfellow, I., et al.: Generative adversarial nets. In: Advances in Neural Information Processing Systems, pp. 2672–2680 (2014)
5. Goodfellow, I.J., Shlens, J., Szegedy, C.: Explaining and harnessing adversarial examples. arXiv preprint arXiv:1412.6572 (2014)
6. Grosse, K., et al.: Adversarial perturbations against deep neural networks for malware classification. arXiv preprint arXiv:1606.04435 (2016)
7. Gu, S., Rigazio, L.: Towards deep neural network architectures robust to adversarial examples. arXiv preprint arXiv:1412.5068 (2014)

8. Kingma, D., Adam, J.B.: A method for stochastic optimization. arXiv preprint arXiv:1412. 6980 (2014)
9. Kolter, J.Z., Maloof, M.A.: Learning to detect malicious executables in the wild. In: Proceedings of the Tenth ACM SIGKDD International Conference on Knowledge Discovery and Data Mining, pp. 470–478. ACM (2004)
10. Kolter, J.Z., Maloof, M.A.: Learning to detect and classify malicious executables in the wild. J. Machine Learn. Res. **7**, 2721–2744 (2006)
11. Li, B., Vorobeychik, Y., Chen, X.: A general retraining framework for scalable adversarial classification. arXiv preprint arXiv:1604.02606 (2016)
12. Liu, Y., Chen, X., Liu, C., Song, D.: Delving into transferable adversarial examples and black-box attacks. arXiv pre-print arXiv:1611.02770 (2016)
13. Microsoft: Microsoft portable executable and common object file format specification (2013)
14. Mirza, M., Osindero, S.: Conditional generative adversarial nets. arXiv preprint arXiv:1411. 1784 (2014)
15. Papernot, N., McDaniel, P., Ian, G.: Transferability in machine learning: from phenomena to black-box attacks using adversarial samples. arXiv preprint arXiv:1605.07277 (2016)
16. Papernot, N., et al.: Practical black-box attacks against deep learning systems using adversarial examples. arXiv preprint arXiv:1602.02697 (2016)
17. Papernot, N., et al.: The limitations of deep learning in adversarial settings. In: Security and Privacy (Eu-roS&P), 2016 IEEE European Symposium on Security and Privacy (EuroS&P), pp. 372–387. IEEE (2016)
18. Papernot, N., et al.: Distillation as a defense to adversarial perturbations against deep neural networks. In: Security and Privacy (SP), 2016 IEEE Symposium on, pp. 582–597. IEEE (2016)
19. Radford, A., Metz, L., Chintala, S.: Unsupervised representation learning with deep convolutional generative adversarial networks. arXiv preprint arXiv:1511.06434 (2015)
20. Salimans, T., et al.: Improved techniques for training gans. In: Advances in Neural Information Processing Systems, pp. 2226– 2234 (2016)
21. Schultz, M.G., Eskin, E., Zadok, E., Stolfo, S.J.: Data mining methods for detection of new malicious executables. In: Security and Privacy, 2001. S&P. Proceedings. 2001 IEEE (2001)
22. Szegedy, C., et al.: Intriguing properties of neural networks. arXiv preprint arXiv:1312.6199 (2013)

Artificial Intelligence Fostering Fintech: Emerging Trends and Use Cases

Ruchika Gupta[1] (ID), Gagan Kukreja[2] (ID), Anish Gupta[3,5(✉)] (ID), and Lalit Tyagi[4] (ID)

[1] Amity University, Greater Noida, India
[2] Ahlia University, Manama, Bahrain
gkukreja@ahlia.edu.bh
[3] ABES Engineering College, Ghaziabad, India
[4] GL Bajaj Institute of Technology and Management, Greater Noida, India
[5] Chandigarh University, Punjab, India

Abstract. Artificial Intelligence has disrupted the Financial Services Industry. The emerging innovations such as, machine learning, artificial intelligence, cryptocurrency, and data mining leave no financial institutions across the globe untouched. These advances have profoundly predisposed several facets of financial markets like investments, transfers, billings, rewards, insurance, remittances, underwriting etc. Fintech companies were the early adopters of these AI powered innovations to promote greater budgetary awareness, human life development, improved decision-making, and more. This paper explores the growth of Fintech in India, its associated challenges, and the opportunities emerging from high penetration, demographic dividend and connectivity to modern and affordable technology, low smartphone rates, and public policies like Digital India, Make in India, etc. Through uses cases of Artificial Intelligence, the paper also elaborates how Artificial Intelligence fosters fintech companies. Lastly, this paper suggests strategies that may help practitioners and researchers to tap the untapped potentials of Fintech in India.

Keywords: Fintech · Artificial Intelligence · Data analytics · Financial innovation · Digitalization · Digital India · Financial inclusion

1 Introduction

Technology has reshaped the finance and financial markets in many ways over the past several decades, including electronic banking, ATM use, online banking, core banking solutions, and many more. Latest technology such as artificial intelligence, deep learning, block chain and data mining leave no financial markets across the globe untouched [1]. Fintech is one such technology that joins inventive plans of action and innovation in order to empower, improve and disturb the financial services industry. It is a fresh jargon term in the 4th world of industrial revolution (Industry 4.0).

© Springer Nature Switzerland AG 2021
R. Agrawal et al. (Eds.): ICCEDE 2020, CCIS 1436, pp. 61–73, 2021.
https://doi.org/10.1007/978-3-030-84842-2_5

Fintech may be referred to as a financial innovation since it encompasses innovative ideas that propose technology solutions to improve financial service processes. These inventive thoughts may likewise prompt new plans of action or even new organizations. Fintech, at its center, expected to help organizations and buyers deal with their money related tasks and cycles in a vastly improved way. It improves end-user experience, eases and automates financial institutions processes.

The term Fintech was coined in 21st century and was initially used for the technologies deployed in the systems used for back end operations in financial institutions. Over the years, the focus has shifted towards inclusion of more consumer oriented services. That's why; many Fintech firms including Paytm (mobile payment) have sought to provide a one-stop solution for all the simple needs of ordinary customers'.

The Fintech industry has developed immensely over the period. At present, the industry is a host of not only startups but also seasoned companies operating on a global stage and offering extensive assortment of financial services in addition to start ups. Moreover, Fintech services adoption has increased significantly, from 16% in 2015 to 33% in 2017, and to 64% in 2019. The global Fintech AI industry is forecast to exceed USD 22.6 billion by 2025. In the forecast timeframe (2020–2025), the demand is also projected to experience a CAGR of 23.37% [2] (Fig. 1).

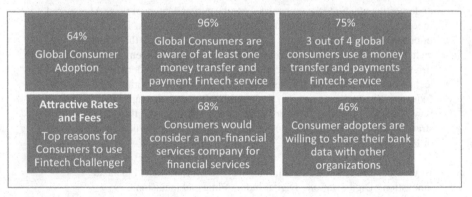

Fig. 1. Global consumer adoption. *Source: EY Global Fintech Adoption Index, 2019* [2]

Further, the broader Fintech category can be segmented into four variants as per McKinsey Analysis [3] (Fig. 2):

Origin	Technology	Infrastructure Providers seeking to help financial institutions digitize and modernize their technology stacks	Large technology ecosystem using financial services to strengthen relationships with users
	Financial Services	New entrants, startups, and attackers seeking to enter financial services using new technologies	Incumbent financial institutions making significant investments in technology to lift their game
		Low	**High**
		Scale	

Fig. 2. Fintech category variants. *Source: McKinsey Analysis, 2018* [3]

2 Need of the Study

Artificial Intelligence is fostering fintech companies by offering technological solutions to the human problems. It not only improves the precision level but also speed up the query resolution period. The union of AI and Fintech generates both disruption and synergies. Moreover, these challenges keep multiplying exponentially with the speedy growth in the adoption of Fintech industry in India. Fintech also plays a crucial role in fulfilling the financial inclusion agenda of the Indian Governments through Aadhar, digital India & unbanked banking. Therefore, there is an imperative need to understand how AI fosters fintech processes so that fintech companies could leverage the potential of AI technologies.

3 Objectives of the Study

The objectives of this study are:

- To analyse the emergence and adoption of Fintech in India;
- To evaluate the challenges faced by various companies during adoption of Fintech;
- To study the impact of Fintech adoption on the financial sector of the country; and
- To assess the emerging trends and the opportunities;
- To demonstrate the implementation of AI in fintech processes by use cases; and
- To suggest strategies to tap the untapped potential of Fintech.

4   Emergence and Adoption of Fintech in India

India started to travel the journey of globalization and liberalization in 1993, when many banks from the private sector entered India and began operations. Beforehand, the banking industry was dominated mainly by the main public sector banks (PSBs). These private sector banks were equipped with latest technologies and soon become a big threat for PSBs.

In 1998, for example, ICICI Bank was the first bank to introduce Net Banking in India, which reduced payment times from 3–5 days to just few hours, cutting lots of time and effort and ameliorating various concerns of businesses functioning in India. From that point forward, Fintech has been step by step developing with digitization beginning after 2010, prompting the dispatch of portable financial applications by banks and giving client banking solace in their grasp and improving client experience over their PCs, cell phones and PCs.

Everything considered Fintech has changed the style of Indian budgetary organizations from paper-based KYC to electronic KYC, enlistment portions to National Electronic Funds Transfer, or an enormous number of wallets made available to clients. India is flourishing in the Fintech division right now and a few new firms/new businesses are thinking of amazingly imaginative things. Whatsapp, google, apple and numerous others started installment frameworks through their Indian applications which are not yet accessible in numerous countries of the world.

The key elements for the fast development of this part are government-driven digitization ventures, strategy changes, system, for example Start-up India Plan, eKYC standards, UPI, Aadhar, Budgetary Consideration, and so on. Such imaginative government approaches put the Indian budgetary market at the worldwide focal point, making a solid stage for Fintech organizations and administrations.

A further basic lift created when India's governing body announced the demonetization of 500- and 1,000-rupee notes on 8 November 2016, and people had no other alternative aside from to mobile wallet or card or bank channel portions that gave the digital payments industry an enormous drive. Paytm was one of the major beneficiaries in this shift in administration. Its user base was about 125 million before demonetization, which rose to 185 million within 3 months. It also expanded in terms of merchant revenue, acquiring 5 million retailers with QR code acceptance in one year, and managing $1.6 billion in three and a half annual transactions [5].

Millions of citizens in India prefer to use mobile payments (99.5%) and within a few days become aware of them for the first time in their lives. As per the 2019 EY Global Fintech Adoption Study distributed on June 3, 2019, India and China have a Fintech Adoption Record of 87% in the principal quarter of 2019, far better in front of other world nations [3, 6, 7]. As shown in a study by PwC and ASSOCHAM, with respect to Fintech adoption, India obtained the second highest spot worldwide at 57.9% [8].

Approximately 42% of Fintech start-ups have hubs in Mumbai and Bangalore, the remainder are spread around and a healthy 12% share is located in the National Capital Region [9]. The organizations that develop in this room can be isolated accurately into 4 divisions, for example Installments, charges, awards and store holding. Payment sector can be partitioned into Digital wallets, Portable POS, Payment Gateways are just a couple of classes where there is a great deal of activity. The fundamental parts around there are Citrus Pay, CCAvenue, PayUBiz India, PayUMoney, JusPay and Transecute. Credits might be separated into distant advances, P2P advances and SME advances, and so forth. Riches the executives is one of the huge locales where numerous organizations concoct new arrangements when the net gain per family has become fundamentally throughout the long term. Subsequently, residents need uphold in making wise speculation decisions [10].

During the initial stages, several of the Fintech startups are financed by Venture Capitalists (VCs), later they infuse multi-million dollars into these businesses based on the market and development of large corporations or investment firms. Fintech is now used as an alternative to mainstream banks and procedures; it is creating automated solutions to existing cash distribution systems. Banks have now started developing things like api banking, electronic account management, e- collections, and many more. These two things hit millennials who consider that Fintech is greater than traditional banking. For eg, a business would be able to provide several account numbers for automated account management and can be exchanged between various customers. Fintech is also being seen as an option to the conventional banks and procedures; it provides digital alternatives for current cash delivery mechanism. Banks have already begun to grow items like upi banking, e-account control, e-collections and several other.

Further, by requesting that banks develop an ever increasing number of POS termi- nals, the legislature has begun taking a few measures to build the entrance of installment terminals. For what it's worth with the BRICS countries, India has the most reduced number of POS terminals, for example 1 POS for each 500 individuals, this demon- strates money related innovation firms like Versatile POS (Paytm, mobikwik and so forth.) have an extensive potential to join this area. The legislature has set up a body called the National Payment Council of India, which propelled an advanced domestic payments framework called Rupay. The main aim of introducing this was to raise rev- enue and monitor in-house purchases that were routed by foreign companies such as Visa or Mastercard. Government has taken a number of measures to encourage it within India and outside India.

During the first quarter of 2019, India has surpassed China as the top FinTech finance target market in Asia with investments of about $286 million over 29 transactions, relative to China's $192.1 million across 29 transactions. Digital Banking, Digital Financing, BankTech, InsurTech, and WealthTech are main segments within the FinTech room [17] (Fig. 3).

$2.4 bn FinTech software market size	$5.7 bn Investments in FinTech (2014-18)	$14.1 bn Digital payments through UPI (2018)	29% Highest expected RoI on Fintech projects globally

Fig. 3. Fintech market in India. *Source: InvestIndia, 2019* [17]

According to a survey by EY [2], awareness and acceptance of fintech in India have skyrocketed in all categories. The report shows that while awareness and acceptance across most categories are high, the bucket of transfers & payments seems to have made the most important inroads. 99.5% of the surveyed customers in India were cognizant of FinTech apps for this form of transaction (Fig. 4).

4% Money Transfer and Payments	29% Budgeting and Financial Planning	22% Savings and Investments	24% Borrowing	14% Insurance

Fig. 4. Consumer awareness of Fintech services in India. *Source: EY Global Fintech Adoption Index, 2019* [2]

5 Adoption Challenges

Though India has the second highest Fintech adoption rate in the world [2], the adoption has faced several challenges which need to be addressed to tap the full potential of such adoption. These are given:-

- **Financial Illiteracy**: Despite launching initiatives like Pradhan Mantri Jan Dhan Yojna, the success rate is too low because of the financial illiteracy amongst people of India. It poses serious challenge for successful Fintech adoption. But now majority of young people are quite adoptive of new technology.
- **Socio-economic disparities**: Though the reliance Jio has disrupted the telecom market and increased the internet penetration, despite the utility of Fintech services in rural India is very low. Yet, it is hoped it will gradually improve and create new opportunities in rural areas.
- **Regulatory Issues**: Regulatory uncertainty in the Fintech sector is making things complicated for both Fintech service providers and consumers. India can learn from China who brought a comprehensive regulation for Fintech in September 2019.
- **Cyber Threats**: Cyber security threats and lack of regulatory mechanisms comes as a major problem for the expansion of services. Legislature of India must think to bring information security guidelines like The General Data Protection Regulation (GDPR) of Europe.
- **Infrastructure Issues**: Relatively weak infrastructure such as underdeveloped payment systems, lack of customer credit data, legal enforcement mechanisms for payment obligations, electricity, weak internet coverage are also another drawback.
- **Conservative Approach of Indian Customers**: Indian customers have been known to have conservative approach with respect to finance which may be seen in their financial preferences. In such a scenario, Fintech companies are required to infuse greater confidence among customers.

6 Impact of Fintech Adoption on the Indian Financial Sector

Fintech is searching for another approach to empower rising business sectors like India experience the advantages of advanced innovations and mean to diminish the holes among rising and industrialized nations. Investigating the Fintech companies' quick development, banks have started to consider opening a Fintech division in the traditional bank. Some business veterans guarantee this is one of India's merciless competition's methods of raising and that on expanding cost of customer procurement.

Mobile banking is one of the spots where banks have started to forcefully connect, whereby a bank works chiefly on an application based stage, where the entire technique for opening a ledger doesn't involve a branch visit and anything can be cultivated on wireless fingertips.

MSME funding is another area in which Fintechs turned up early pledge. The field is seeing new Fintech emerge players that fix the systemic problems in asymmetry in details as well as reducing processing times for small loans. Fintech is now committed to reducing prices, Credit, particularly by reducing lenders' operating expenses. Lower due diligence expenses and running costs for improved KYC procedures spending.

Fintech seems to have the ability to affect Governance in various aspects. Firstly, Fintech has the ability to bring clarity if the demand for cash is diminished and more purchases are made, this can be best tracked by digital means. Additionally, more business practices and an enhanced one growing the government's tax base to boost the labour market spending. Third, the increase in economic activity may reduce informal market size by promoting and supporting businesses by governments officials.

Fintech's possible effect on different stakeholders involves, but not limited to:

- A culture of innovation and entrepreneurship,
- Better financial inclusion prospects,
- The growth of Tech-enabled Non-Banking Financing Firms,
- Improved consumer financial management quality,
- KYC Process Converted,
- Credit evaluation theoretically allowed,
- Simplified Small to Medium Business goods & facilities,
- Improved choices for controlling capital,
- Revolutionizing regular payment collection,
- Reduced insurer liability and uncertainty,
- Reduced defensive unpredictability and ambiguity,
- Make money transfer quicker and more convenient,
- Faster and increasingly stable movements in currency,
- Knowledge search and block chain for convenience, and
- New financial models such as neobanks, cloud banking and the sky are the limit from that stage.

7 Emerging Trends and Opportunities

Expert financial tools, AI algorithms, and SaaS technologies have played a crucial role in growing the growth of Fintech and will also improve Fintech in future. Emerging markets like Insurtech, Proptech, Wealthtech, and Regtech would gain the skills from the latest Fintech products and services. Maybe both businesses will merge and offer innovative imaginative product products and services together. The eventual fate of Fintech glances energizing especially in rising and crowded economies like India, where 65% of the populace is under 35 years old and simply 0.4 dependence proportion. Obviously this means that the demand for modern specialized products and services solutions will be high with the engaged population.

The administration set an objective of $4 billion or more advanced exchanges, which it neglected to reach in 2018. The controller (RBI) and government backing will in this manner be strong, and would be available to creative thoughts. In the amazingly various nation's serious condition with 22 authority dialects and 10,000 or more neighborhood tongues, organizations, money related ventures, lawmakers, and business visionaries may consider how to enter and develop the account or digital payments industry. Traditional banks face several obstacles, such as determining which company's loan should be approved and which it should be refused, resulting in lots of unstable properties. With cutting edge information investigation apparatuses the creditors\' potential issues can be anticipated ahead of time. Government and banks cannot continue to run the presentation like this, so the Fintech will play an indispensable situation with delicate human intercession in the destiny of saves money with tremendous non-performing credits.

Research & Development is indeed one of the main fields that several businesses can concentrate on the constantly evolving environment over the next several decades. The emerging economy such as India would rise at a much faster rate about 6 and 8% relative to what has been witnessed so far by the United States or any other industrialized nation. The greatest test for Fintech is hold its inventive laborers/minds, provided that this isn't taken care of, Indian Fintech would end up being not so good in view of cerebrum channel, on the grounds that created nations will fire purchasing up the best Indian cerebrums to make something in their own nations and sell it back to India at a cost that would make a mark in the nation\'s universal currency reserves.

In order to satisfy the increasing demand in the coming years, Fintech firms will have to rely more on artificial intelligence and machine learning [11, 12]. Any of the firms have already moved in this path and have begun robotic advice in the wealth technology room with a gentle human hand. Predictive analytics would also be a turning point in Fintech's future, as the analysis of human activity would be the main field of focus in targeting, selling and designing new creative technologies.

Most notably, many Indians are still reliant on agriculture/farming as a main profession, for a productive future they will need a hybrid of agrotech combined with Fintech. Government has taken financial inclusion seriously in the last couple of years that will enable farmers incorporate emerging technologies in their banking transactions. Fintech firms would need to concentrate on creating portable first methodology items contrasted with different channels since most Indians invest more energy in their telephones than the remainder of their computerized gadgets. May be better with mobile phones. The change from 4G to 5G, the new corporate assessment decrease [13], government activity toward organization and less expensive mobiles will speed up and ease later on in this segment. It will be simpler to achieve first portable arrangement since India has the most minimal cost per giga byte of information around the world. That will go about as an impetus to Fintech [14].

A huge number of provincial Indians are ready interpersonal interaction firms, for example, Facebook, Instagram and so on, which straightforwardly shows that whatever is anything but difficult to get a handle on and has a nice UI, client experience would be utilized by most Indian individuals. Free (though restricted) government-provided Wi-Fi empowers shoppers to get to more web innovation [13]. Block Chain wasn't famous in India till now, however with the gigantic increment in the quantity of Indians traveling to another country just because, the level of presentation would be very high and the focal points will be appreciated by the Fintech organizations who concoct an answer who satisfies the needs of worldwide Indians.

8 Artificial Intelligence in Fintech: Use Cases

Artificial Intelligence is improvising the various fintech processes in the way they are implemented and processed. Some of the use cases of Artificial Intelligence are given:

o **Automated Customer Support Services**: Chatbots and computer based intelligence interfaces like Cleo, Eno, and the Wells Fargo Bot connect with clients and answer inquiries, offering enormous potential to cut front office and helpline staffing costs. Natural Language Preparing (NLP) is actually the key here – using profound learning calculations to get language and produce reactions in an increasingly regular manner. Swedbank, which has over a portion of its clients previously utilizing computerized banking, is utilizing the Nina chatbot with NLP to attempt and completely resolve 2 million value-based calls to its contact place every year [15, 16].
o **Financial Frauds Detection**: AI is the cutting-edge technology used to combat financial fraud. In a matter of seconds ML algorithms will evaluate millions of data points to detect anomalous transactional trends. If such questionable actions are identified, it is simple to decide if they were only errors that were created by the acceptance process or signs of a malicious operation in any form. Mastercard is releasing the newest Decision Intelligence (DI) platform to evaluate growing customer's past payment data to identify and deter real-time credit card fraud. Data Advisor is a company which uses AI to detect a common form of cybercrime based on taking advantage of new payment card accounts sign-up incentives [15].
o **Risk Profiling and Credit Score**: Many people may not have adequate credit background because their credit score is small. As a consequence, the banks are not taking the chance of lending them capital. Perfectly trustworthy individuals who will pay back loans may not get loans because of this. This is an environment where the FinTech firms are providing consumers with AI-powered solutions. Lenddo, a FinTech company located in Singapore, utilizes AI algorithms to evaluate alternate data points to assess a prospective borrower's credit-worthiness. Users signing up with Lenddo would enable the app to mine their social networking info, web browsers, geo-locations, smartphones, etc. Lenddo's AI algorithms evaluate various factors and assess the credit value.

o **Preventing Cyber Threats**: New artificial intelligence controlled systems, for example, Global Intelligence Network of DataVisor have been created to dissuade digital assaults, extending from social control, secret word showering, and login stuffing to unadulterated seizing by PC. This stage can gather and total gigantic measures of information including IP addresses, topographical areas, email spaces, and so forth. Upon digested, this vast data collection is evaluated to identify any unusual behavior, and then to deter or resolve takeovers of account [16].

o **Action towards Money Laundering**: The revelation of recently revealed illegal tax avoidance exercises and fear monger financing systems is perhaps the best issue banks face far and wide. When identifying dubious occurrences, machine learning algorithms and artificial neural networks reliably outflank any traditional measurable framework. In conjunction with big data analytics, the business Theta Ray used sophisticated unsupervised ML algorithms to evaluate various data points, such as recent consumer activity and historical behaviour [16].

o **Quantitative Trading:** The method of using broad data sets to find trends that might be used to make successful trades is quantitative trading. In this mode of trade, artificial intelligence is particularly useful. Computers powered by AI can process massive, complex data sets quicker and more effectively than humans. Trades are automated by the subsequent algorithmic trading processes and save precious time. Alpha Sense is an AI-powered search engine for the finance industry and represents clients such as banks, brokerage firms and Fortune 500 businesses. To uncover developments and patterns in financial markets, the app uses natural language analysis to examine keyword queries inside filings, documents, analysis, and news [18].

o **Helpful in Account Reconciliation:** Practically each organisation has to face some sort of account reconciliation problem as it is an excessively repetitive and cumbersome operation that has to be done manually or through Excel-based procedures. Over this, inaccuracies are much too frequent, particularly though the rule-based methods solve this issue. In reality, they appear to breakdown as the code shifts or new use cases are implemented and require on-going support, rather than being incredibly costly to set up due to complex machine configuration and coding. SigmaIQ created its own engine of reconciliation based on machine learning techniques. The device can interpret data on a comparatively greater level, providing a higher degree of faith in pairing, and is able to benefit from feedback [18].

o **Augmented Reality based Research Methods:** A substantial amount of time is spent conducting research in investment finance. Progressed NLP methods will allow a scientist to examine monetary reports easily within a company. Drawing out key points where the firm is most passionate about. Other techniques in data science, such as sentiment analysis, augmented reality etc. may also plan and normalize fiscal summaries [19].

o **Agreement Analyzer:** In the money market, it is a repetitive interior errand. This usual assignment to an AI model may be appointed by managers and counsellors. Optical character recognition (OCR) may be used to digitize the archives of scanned originals. It will then be feasible for an NLP model with layered business logic to easily decode, register, and write agreements. The strength of this use of simulated intelligence has been saddled by JP Morgan, causing 360,000 h (yearly) to be released from the heap of its employees in just a few moments [19].

9 Conclusion

Fintech has grown gradually in the underlying years however this room has seen a fast radical development over the most recent four years on account of the favorable to digitization activities of the Indian government. On account of the expansion in India's dynamic populace and increasing education rates, it will keep on ascending at an uncommon pace in the following twenty years. The resistive response of the Bank to these improvements will likewise assume a key job in the far reaching and quick multiplication of Fintech [4].

Currently, it only takes a few hours to finish the whole lending process, and if one applies for a lending in the morning, the loan funds are paid off on the same day. In comparison, both precision and pace have improved with the introduction of Amnesty International into the multifaceted financial market. Artificial Intelligence, together with big data and predictive analytics, is now very successful in growing the scope and scale of financial institutions around the globe, from selling the goods and services to consumer analysis.

Fintech centers across the alchemy of expertise, intellect and automation. For fintech companies that use it to develop credit risk assessments, activity and pattern detection and fraud applications, AI is going to be the key differentiator. This will encourage them to gain an advantage over their competitors. Via different instruments and algorithms, AI will make a difference in future banking and financial services. Some of the organizational touch points for this include: onboarding consumers to minimize processing time dependent on credit and social media for decision making, Chatbots and robotic advisors to instigate customized and informative communications, enabling workflow management for corporate activities such as paper preparation and activity replication through divisions, managing the supply chain, and mitigating product pilfering to mention a few.

Though, adjustment to new technologies is a regular challenge, but providing services or goods according to consumer demands is the secret to a profitable enterprise. FinTech companies are also tailoring themselves to the demands of emerging economies like India. In particular, they are working hard to build a financial system that is more customer-friendly by removing all paperwork ambiguity and supplying goods.

To conclude, FinTech has enormous growth potential and the vast level of the underserved population is proof that we should foresee a transformation special to the subcontinent. The FinTech industry in India has the scope and creativity to globalize and establish a strong footprint in an interdependent world.

10 Recommendations

India, being such a nation including 1.3 billion individuals, request and flexibly will keep on being an issue, the organization that can prevail with regards to fulfilling the requests of a bigger extent of the populace. While this doesn't generally infer that the claim to fame items would come up short, they should decide whether their purchasers will manage the cost of the value they intend to sell at, or in the event that they will fall not long after the delivery. So as to make things simpler and successful, the following recommendations are made:

- The Fintech companies should make themselves able to cope up with the language barrier especially for the country having multiple regional languages.
- The UI and client experience ought to be the essential region of center and ought not be disregarded at any expense.
- Infrastructure issues needs to be addressed for the expansion of services.
- These companies should be backed by sustainable business models.
- Policies need to be formulated so as to mitigate potential risks and fostering the benefits.
- Government should set the platform for smooth operations of start-ups with favorable policies and tax incentives specific to the Fintech sector.

References

1. Kumar, B., Ghai, R., Tyagi, M., Gupta, R.: Leveraging technology for robust financial facilities: a comparative assessment of BRICS nations. In: International Conference on Computation, Automation and Knowledge Management (ICCAKM), pp. 481–486, Dubai, United Arab Emirates (2020), https://doi.org/10.1109/ICCAKM46823.2020.9051508
2. Global Fintech Adoption Index. https://assets.ey.com/content/dam/ey-sites/ey-com/en_gl/topics/banking-and-capital-markets/ey-global-Fintech-adoption-index.pdf (2019)
3. McKinsey: Synergy and disruption: ten trends shaping Fintech. https://www.mckinsey.com/industries/financial-services/our-insights/synergy-and-disruption-ten-trends-shaping-Fintech (2018)
4. KPMG: Fintech in India: powering a digital economy. https://assets.kpmg/content/dam/kpmg/in/pdf/2018/09/Fintech_2018.pdf (2018)
5. Wright. C.: How Paytm went big on Indian demonetization. https://www.euromoney.com/article/b15ts6qpxvj51d/how-paytm-went-big-on-indian-demonetization?copyrightInfo=true (2017)
6. Singh, G., Kumar, B., Gupta, R.: Role of consumer's innovativeness & perceived ease of use to engender adoption of digital wallets in India. In: ICACE2018, IEEE Xplore, pp. 150–158 (2018)
7. Varma, S., Gupta, R.: Customer perception and behavioral intention to adopt biometric enabled e-banking services in India, pp. 137–146. Business Analytics and Cyber Security Management in Organizations, IGI Global Publications (2016)
8. Assocham & PwC: Emerging technologies disrupting the financial sector. https://www.pwc.in/assets/pdfs/consulting/financial-services/Fintech/publications/emerging-technologies-disrupting-the-financial-sector.pdf (2019)
9. Sahni, A.: Which are the most successful Fintech startups in India? https://inc42.com/features/which-are-the-most-successful-Fintech-startups-in-india/ (2019)
10. Agarwal, N., Kumar, P.: Reflection on the new innovations for maximizing the learning in teacher of mathematics. Int. J. Educ. Herald, **38**(2), 41. ISSN: 0974-0732 (2009)
11. Gupta, A., Salau, A.O., Chaturvedi, P., Akinola, S.A., Nwulu, N.I.: Artificial neural networks: its techniques and applications to forecasting. In: IEEE International Conference on Automation, Computational and Technology Management (ICACTM), pp. 320–324, London, United Kingdom (2019), https://doi.org/10.1109/ICACTM.2019.8776701
12. Chandra, G., Gupta, R., Agarwal, N.: Role of artificial intelligence in transforming the justice delivery system in COVID 19 pandemic. Int. J. Emerg. Technol. **11**(3), 344–350 (2020)

13. The Economic Times. The Jio effect: consumers have been the absolute winners. https://economictimes.indiatimes.com/articleshow/65694564.cms?utm_source=contentofinterest&utm_medium=text&utm_campaign=cppst (2018)
14. Wee, R.Y.: Which country has the largest number of cellphones? https://www.worldatlas.com/articles/10-countries-with-the-highest-rates-of-cell-phone-subscriptions.html (2019)
15. Agarwal, M.: What impact has India's Fintech ecosystem created on banking? https://inc42.com/features/what-impact-has-indias-Fintech-ecosystem-created-on-banking/ (2019)
16. Papadopoulos, A.: Most start-up friendly countries in the world, 2019. https://ceoworld.biz/2019/01/02/most-startup-friendly-countries-in-the-world-2019/ (2019)
17. https://www.investindia.gov.in/sector/bfsi-fintech-financial-services
18. https://builtin.com/artificial-intelligence/ai-finance-banking-applications-companies
19. https://towardsdatascience.com/ten-applications-of-ai-to-fintech-22d626c2fdac

Security Resilience in Contemporary Applications

Improving Smart Healthcare Safety
and Security Using Kinect

Vijai Singh[1($\boxtimes$)], Neetesh Saxena[2], Drashti Pathak[3], Garima Saini[3],
and Divya Bhatnagar[3]

[1] Department of CSE, G.L. Bajaj Institute of Technology and Management, Gr Noida, India
[2] School of Computer Science and Informatics, Cardiff University, Wales, UK
nsaxena@ieee.org
[3] Department of CSE, IMS Engineering College, Ghaziabad, India

Abstract. Modern healthcare operating rooms are cumbersome, especially in the current pandemic of Coronavirus (COVID-19) to manage the safety and security of the patients and the staff. Conditions in a modern operating room are like, a patient's medical diagnosis or x-ray or the MRI images are the vital resources to be considered. In general, the doctors are impelled to scrub out their hands every time they scroll through or examine the images in mid-operation. To avoid departing the operating table, several doctors put their faith in assistants or nurses and ask to examine the system that can be clumsy and disappointing and can rise the gathering in the room itself. To overcome this problem and emphasizing the use of the touchless smart healthcare system in medical diagnosis we have developed an application for the same. We propose and demonstrate a gesture and speech-based system to help staff to deal with such critical conditions. The proposed system is composed of two main parts: the healthcare operating software and sensor Microsoft Kinect. Test results conclude the efficiency of the viewing system in terms of time complexity, and the value and the safety of the recording system have increased.

Keywords: Kinect · Safety · Touchless · 3D scanning · Bioprinting

1 Introduction

Advancements in technology have led the researchers to develop systems for medical applications especially in the surgical environment [1]. Surgical procedures have become increasingly dependent on a variety of digital imaging systems for navigation, documentation and diagnosis. The necessity to analyze and examine these images during surgical procedures proposed some barriers demanding the need to maintain a sterile surgical environment, especially under the current Coronavirus (COVID-19) pandemic. Maintaining sterility in the operating room is of utmost importance to deal with the safety and security of the healthcare staff in addition to the right treatment given to the patients. Hence, a controlled environment is crucial to minimize the risks which are likely to prevail. Traditional input machines like keyboard, touchscreen, mouse, etc. are dependent

© Springer Nature Switzerland AG 2021
R. Agrawal et al. (Eds.): ICCEDE 2020, CCIS 1436, pp. 77–88, 2021.
https://doi.org/10.1007/978-3-030-84842-2_6

upon physical contact. Howsoever, such contact-based interaction poses a danger for the transfer of contaminated materials. To maintain a sterile environment in operating rooms as well as to avoid scrubbing, doctors rely upon their assistants who help them out in controlling the equipment as well as manipulating the images. But this may sometimes lead to an increase in operating time, errors, and chances of failures. Researches and surveys carried out depict that these practices might lead to chaos and risk to the patient's life. Recently, a touchless interaction device named Kinect was launched by Microsoft in 2010. As shown in Fig. 1, the proposed system makes the use of this device and tries to minimize the loopholes and discrepancies as mentioned above. It provides an efficient and good alternate to doctors. In this direction, researchers have discussed ways and means of smart touchless healthcare [2].

Fig. 1. Kinect setup in healthcare [3].

Contributions: The scenario in a modern operating room is very cumbersome these days. Hence, good technologies that are reliable as well as efficient are in great demand, especially in the current pandemic of COVID-19 to look after the safety and security of the patients as well as the healthcare staff at the same time. Although new techniques have come up in the medical domain for the ease of doctors, still most of the work is done manually. This type of system, which operates via gestures and speech, is not currently in implementation. The proposed system is developed basically to help doctors to deal with conditions in the modern operating room. To control the video, doctors can touch the system physically or just wave their hands. Furthermore, video commands (such as play, pause, stop, volume up, and volume down) can be controlled by speech for smooth and efficient controls. The advantages of this system are (i) minimizing the need of supporting staff in operating rooms, (ii) access to the real-time video (assistance), and (iii) recording of important data for doctors' assistance to avoid inaccuracy in data. To overcome that speech to text conversion features is also one of the requirements of the system [10]. Kinect can act as a 3D scanner and scanned copies of organs can later be 3D printed and act as organs for organ transplants. We demonstrate that if this idea is successfully brought into implementation can work more efficiently compared to the presently used system.

2 Related Work

This section presents existing work related to the healthcare operating room. Saxena et al. [4] developed a proof-of-concept prototype NHealthIoT testbed and shown its usability. Yadav et al. [5] discussed cursor movement by hand gesture and proposed a healthcare application that requires only a simple webcam for implementation. For recognition based on hand gesture, there are generally two main approaches, one is hardware-based and the other one is vision-based. It uses a data glove to achieve gesture recognition. The proposed system effectively eliminated the necessity for a mouse pad [5].

Pei Xu described a Human-Computer Interaction (HCI) system and a recognition-based on hand gesture that are working in real-time [6]. Human-computer interaction, gesture recognition and hand detection are the three components of the proposed system. Preprocessing of images is the first step and thereafter a hand-based detector was attempted to filter the hand image on this image itself. A Convolutional Neural Network (CNN) classifier has been integrated with the Kalman estimator to recognize gestures from the processed image. Finally, the output results are submitted to a control center in order to decide the good probabilistic model [6]. Authors have used Microsoft Kinect for hand detection and gesture recognition to simulate the mouse events. There are two methodology glove-based and vision-based that have been studied. The main disadvantage is the cost of the devices used. However, a more natural way of HCI is offered by a vision-based approach as no physical contact is required. The major drawback of this approach is occlusion [21]. Sawai and Shandilya [14] reviewed gesture and speech recognition using the Kinect device and explored algorithms for the Kinect sensor. They have studied Kinect's gesture recognition, microphone-based speech recognition, and tracking of objects and 3D mapping. A system is built to identify and understand gestures and speech using Kinect sensors. Due to the limitation of the short distance between the human operator and the phone device, voice control still suffers from inconvenient operations. Presently voice control by Kinect voice sensing provides a way that human operators can control the phone device without carrying it far away from the user. McKay and Clement [12] investigated the application of Microsoft Kinect for recognition of visual-only automatic speech and reviewed the ability of Kinect. They tried to use Kinect as an automatic speech recognizer. A program is implemented to identify spoken words and report confidence with which the words are recognized to test the ability of Kinect. They stated that Microsoft Kinect API gives 90% of accuracy for the word recognition system made by them.

Tiangang et al. [20] highlighted 3D surface reconstruction based on the Kinect sensor. They described the 3-D reconstruction route. There are four steps, starting with the preprocessing of data. After this pose estimation of the sensor, fusion of the depth data, and finally, extraction of a 3D surface. Authors in [7] presented results on fusion 4D with real-time observations and then formed a method that establishes incremental restorations to enhance the surface estimation over the period, and parametrizing non-inflexible scene motion. They merged the concept of volumetric fusion and estimation of the smooth deformation field across RGBD views. This method is extremely vigorous to topology changes and also large frames to frame motion, permitting recreating exceptionally difficult scenes. The main advantage of this technique is that it either distorts an online produced template or continually combines intensity data non-firmly into a particular position model. The frame to frame motions will be imprecisely anticipated or the non-inflexible orientation will not succeed to congregate for slow frame rate and large frame to frame motion.

Casino et al. [13] described the approach of using recommendation systems to offer healthcare services so that citizens could collaborate within the city to upgrade their value of life. Sholla et al. [15] presented a new approach that incorporates ethics in IoT based connected smart healthcare. Jangra et al. A multilayered framework [16] has been proposed to enhance the utilities of biosensor-based data collection and aggregation. Alabdulatif et al. [17] demonstrate a framework by evaluating a case study for the patient biosignal data. Authors in [18] proposed a system to enhance the capabilities of IoT-based healthcare systems with fast response time and low latency. Pathinarupothi et al. [19] introduced a smart edge system based on IoT-based to handle remote monitoring of the patients where data is transmitted to software engines using wearable vital sensors. D. Webster and O. Celik [31] reviewed applications of Kinect sensor for elderly care and stroke rehabilitation. They have presented a Systematic review of different Kinect applications.

Kinect sensor is also used in many other applications such as Interactive Educational Technology [23, 28], gesture recognition system designed for severe intellectual disabilities [27, 29], motor rehabilitation [24, 30], etc. Researchers have put in enormous efforts in developing methods for diagnosis and intervention for children with Autism [22, 25, 26].

3 Preliminaries: KINECT

Microsoft launched Kinect, which is a line of motion sensing input devices for Xbox 360 as shown in Fig. 2. In Xbox 360 Microsoft Kinect there is a small motor working as the base to enable the device to be tilted in a horizontal direction is attached to the flat box. The important components of Kinect are mainly infrared (IR) emitter, color camera, tilt motor, LED, microphone array and IR depth sensor.

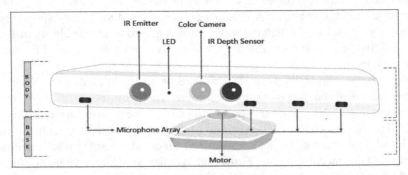

Fig. 2. Kinect device model.

A stream of colored pixels has been captured by the Kinect along with data about pixels. The value of each pixel represents the distance from the sensor to an object in that direction [21]. Thus, Kinect provides developers a means to create an application based on touchless experience through gesture, voice and movement.

4 Proposed Methodology

The proposed system uses the Kinect sensor. The Kinect sensor mainly consists of three parts:

- For capturing the color images an RGB camera is used which stores three-channel data in a 1280 × 960 resolution.
- An IR depth sensor and an infrared (IR) emitter.
- A multi-array microphone, which consists of 4 microphones for capturing sound. We can record audio and also find the direction and location of the sound source.

4.1 Using Kinect to Control the System Cursor

The system cursor is controlled by gesture recognition. Gesture recognition is implemented in the following phases:

- First, the skeletal joints are recognized by Kinect and are sent as input data to the system.
- Next, this joint data is used to recognize certain gestures.
- The recognized gesture is then interpreted to perform the task mapped to it.

In the proposed system, two mouse events namely mouse click and mouse motion are implemented. This is done by mapping mouse coordinates for mouse motion with one of the hands and mapping the click event with the other hand. To implement this, the depth image has been sent to the host device by the Kinect sensor and software implemented on the host works on the decoding of information present in an image. Before the cursor is assigned to the hands and moved, some messages are sent to the control inputs. The X and Y position of the cursor has been assigned after recognition of a user's hand. If the left hand is mapped to the mouse movement and the right one is mapped to click event, then the distance between the left wrist and the left shoulder is obtained and is scaled accordingly with the mouse coordinates. The distance between the left wrist and the left shoulder is obtained if the distance is less than 0.2f (threshold value), the left-click event is raised.

Gesture recognition using Kinect can also be used for posture recognition, fall detection, security and surveillance in modern healthcare operating rooms. This can be done by using one or more cameras, intruder detectors and communication devices to notify alarms. We can also use high end PC which makes it suitable for real-time security.

4.2 Speech Recognition

Microsoft Kinect contains a set of microphone array which acts as voice receiver for performing speech recognition, as shown in Fig. 3. The data acquired by these sensors will be recombined into a single set of voice data. The developer first needs to add the voice command keywords in the grammar (XML) file before they can be recognized. The data will be continuously received by sensors until data involves voice control command keywords as stated in the grammar file of the code running behind these sensors. The Kinect's speech recognition is used in command mode i.e. in this mode command is said and the speech is recognized by the speech recognition engine (SRE). For example, one may want to play or pause a video by just saying "start" and "wait". To develop any speech-enabled application, one typically performs the following basic steps:

- Kinect audio source has been enabled.
- Capturing the audio data stream.
- Identification and starting of the SRE.
- Attach the speech audio source to the recognizer.
- Registration of the event handler.
- Finally, handling the different events invoked by the SRE.

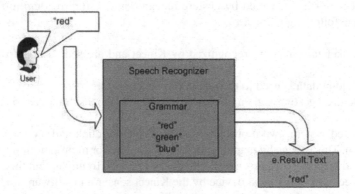

Fig. 3. Speech recognizer grammar.

4.3 3D Scanning of Real Objects

For scanning of real-world objects, Kinect can act as a 3D scanner. Microsoft Kinect has been used in the proposed system which provides 3D object scanning and model creation. By integration of depth data taken from Kinect sensors over time from various viewpoints, the dense surface models are reconstructed into smooth surfaces. By moving either the object or the Kinect sensor the multiple viewpoints of objects are fused to give a single reconstruction voxel volume. As the sensor is moved around, various scenes are integrated to create the 3D model. The first stage of scanning the 3D models of real objects is the depth map conversion. Raw depth data from Xbox 360 Kinect is taken and then converted into floating-point depth in meters. The surface normal at these points are used with AllignedPointCloud functions.

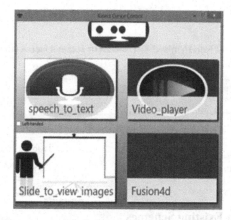

Fig. 4. Kinect system interface control for the experiment setup.

A Kinect system interface control has shown in Fig. 4. Global camera pose is calculated in the second stage and pose has been tracked when the sensor moves in each frame. So, the current sensor pose relative to the initial starting frame is always known by the system. Kinect Fusion has two algorithms:

- NUI FusionAlignPointClouds
- AlignDepthToReconstruction

The third stage is the fusing of depth data with a running average to reduce noise. In this step, the integration of depth data is implemented per frame. It also handles some dynamic changes in the scene. With this, we get a.obj file of the scanned 3-D module. This obj file of the scanned organ is imported into the mesh lab and some enhancements could be performed on it. 3D bioprinting of the scanned organ could be performed and hence can be used for transplantation.

5 Performance Analysis

This section discusses the performance efficiency of the proposed approach with traditional manual work.

5.1 Comparison with Manual Work

To scan through patients' reports and medical records, there are two ways, i.e., via traditional means the one that includes physical touch and the other one is the system which has been proposed to avoid physical touch.

As shown in Table 1, the average time for each user was recorded to be 1.78 s., 1.48 s. and 1.59 s., respectively, using the proposed system. The time of 1.48 s. is found to be the minimal delay when compared to the removal of scrubs recorded at 16.07 s. This is considered an improvement to the time efficiency of the operation. The total average time for this analysis comes out to be 1.61 s., which gives reasonable results.

Table 1. Average User Time

Trials	User-1 (in sec.)	User-2 (in sec.)	User-3 (in sec.)
1	1.72	1.34	1.78
2	2.94	1.52	1.46
3	1.30	1.58	1.61
4	1.24	1.38	1.45
5	1.72	1.62	1.68
Average	1.78	1.48	1.59

5.2 Comparison with Existing Schemes

For gesture and action recognition, there are many approaches proposed by researchers. Using the MEMS inertial sensors, we were able to:

- Miniaturize any delay as they are lightweight.
- Reduced overall cost, as the cost of such sensors, has actually been dropping.
- Utilize them for capturing the movement of a human in real unconstrained environments to find accurate results.
- Use for near real-time feedback.

However, Kinect comes with an RGB color camera and a depth sensor, which provide us with gesture recognition along with full-body 3D motion capture capabilities in the form of skeleton points. Real-time feedback can also be obtained using Microsoft Kinect. This new advance technology is widely being used due to the following reasons:

- There is no requirement for body sensors.
- Skeleton data can be extracted using software such as OpenNI and Kinect SDK.

Thus, due to the above-mentioned reasons using Kinect or other such cameras proves to be better while implementing a gesture recognition system compared to any wearable technology. The gesture recognition was compared with other state-of-the-art methods to evaluate the advantages and disadvantages of this method. The system is compared with [8, 9] and [11]. In [8] the author advised a method based on the ZCam and an SVM-SMO classifier. Furthermore, in [9], the authors proposed the hand gesture recognition system using a range camera with a satisfactory real-time ability. Motion tracking has been combined with the mean-shift algorithm to capture the hand gestures in [11].

5.3 Results and Discussion

The system benefits medical fields and communities by making the operation process more efficient and keeps it in an aseptic and sterile condition with an added benefit of reduced time consumption. It increases the efficiency as well as reliability thereby, saving much of the doctor's time as well as supporting staff required. The system was also subjected for examination by Doctors from a renowned hospital where it was appreciated and was found beneficial by the surgeons themselves.

Table 2 presents comparative experimental results between the contact system and the touchless system. The traditional contact system includes attributes such as removal of scrubs (16.07 s.), changing of plates (8.00 s.), walk for or viewing room/area (18.8 s.), and re-scrubbing (26.17 s.). Whereas the modern contactless system includes program startup (5.38 s.), detection of gestures (1.52 s.), image flow view startup (16.7 s.), and image flow view startup (26.1 s.). Observing from Table 2, the touchless system outperforms the traditional contact system.

This work also compares the proposed technique with the methods proposed in [8, 9], and [11]. This comparison is presented in Table 3 where the average recognition accuracy and miss rate are computed for those methods. The values of average recognition accuracy for methods [8, 9, 11], and proposed method are 0.78, 0.74, 0.77, and 0.85, respectively, whereas the miss rate values for these methods are 0.18, 0.20, 0.16, and 0.14, respectively.

Table 2. Experimental results: contact vs. touchless system

Contact system (in Sec.)				
	Test-1	Test-2	Test-3	Avg.
Removal of scrubs	15.4	14.6	18.2	16.07
Changing of plates	7.36	8.25	8.4	8.00
Viewing room	16.7	20.4	19.3	18.8
Rescrubbing	24.6	28.4	25.5	26.17
Touchless system (in Sec.)				
	Test-1	Test-2	Test-3	Avg.
Program startup	5.35	5.77	5.03	5.38
Detection of gestures	1.52	1.71	1.34	1.52
Image flow view startup	15.8	12.8	21.4	16.7
Image flow view startup	27.2	26.4	24.8	26.1

Table 3. Comparison of kinect with other methods

Method	Average recognition accuracy	Miss rate
[8]	0.78	0.18
[9]	0.74	0.20
[11]	0.77	0.16
Proposed method	0.85	0.14

6 Conclusion and Future Work

The current scenario of the COVID-19 pandemic really demands highly efficient techniques and procedures to handle a large number of patients per day for several months around the world. The proposed approach very much falls under the scope of the current healthcare situation. The proposed system is developed basically to help doctors to deal with conditions in modern operating room. This system minimizes the need of supporting staff in operating rooms. Sometimes doctors also need real time video assistance. The proposed system will help to eliminate the traditionally used interaction methods with the system by eliminating physical contact or any wearable technology, which is one of the key requirements today. Ultimately, the system proves to be beneficial in medical fields and to the community by making the operational process more efficient and also keeps it an aseptic and sterile condition with an added benefit of reduced time consumption. The proposed system can be further improved with time in the future to enhance other healthcare applications including stroke rehabilitation to recover stroke patients, fall prevention in elders is about predicting and preventing falls in the elderly.

References

1. Bansal, M., Gandhi, B.: IoT based development boards for smart healthcare applications. In: 4th International Conference on Computing Communication and Automation (ICCCA), pp. 1–7, (2018)
2. Zhu, H.: Smart healthcare in the era of internet-of-things. IEEE Cons. Electron. Magazine **8**(5), 26–30 (2019)
3. Microsoft Ads showcase social impact of kinect, Nov. 2011. [Online]. https://www.campaignlive.co.uk/article/microsoft-ads-showcase-social-impact-kinect/1101648
4. Saxena, D., Raychoudhury, V.: Design and verification of an NDN-based safety-critical application: a case study with smart healthcare. IEEE Transac. Syst. Man Cybernetics: Syst. **49**(5), 991–1005 (2019)
5. Yadav, O., Makhwana, S., Yadav, P.: Cursor movement by hand gesture. Int. J. Eng. Sci. Res Technol. **6**(3), 234–237 (2017)
6. Xu, P.: A real-time hand gesture. Recogn. Hum.-Comput. Interact. Syst., **1–8** (2017). [Online]. https://arxiv.org/pdf/1704.07296.pdf
7. Dou, M., Khamis, S., Degtyarev, Y., Davidson, P., Fanello, S.R.: Fusion4D: real-time performance capture of challenging scenes. In: SIGGRAPH, pp. 1–13 (2015)
8. Lucas, B.: 3D hand gesture recognition using a ZCAM and an SVMSMO classifier. Graduate Theses and Dissertations. Paper 10829 (2009)
9. Li, Z., Jarvis, R.: Real time hand gesture recognition using a range camera. In: Australasian Conference on Robotics and Automation, pp. 1–7 (Dec. 2009)
10. Gowing, M., Ahmadi, A., Destelle, F., Monaghan, D.S., O'Connor, N.E., Moran, K.: Kinect vs. low-cost inertial sensing for gesture recognition. In: Gurrin, C., Hopfgartner, F., Hurst, W., Johansen, H., Lee, H., O'Connor, N. (eds.) MMM 2014. LNCS, vol. 8325, pp. 484–495. Springer, Cham (2014). https://doi.org/10.1007/978-3-319-04114-8_41
11. Lahamy, H., Lichti, D.D.: Evaluation of real-time hand motion tracking using a range camera and the mean-shift algorithm. Internat. Arch. Photogrammetry, Remote Sens. Spatial Inform. Sci. **38**(6), 139–144 (2011)
12. McKay, P., Clement, B., Haverty, S., Newton, E., Butler, K.: Read my lips: towards use of the Microsoft Kinect as a visual-only automatic speech recognizer. In: Workshop on Home Usable Privacy and Security, pp. 1–5, Nov. 2014

13. Casino, F., Patsakis, C., Batista, E., Postolache, O., Martínez-Ballesté, A., Solanas, A.: Smart healthcare in the IoT era: a context-aware recommendation example. In: International Symposium in Sensing and Instrumentation in IoT Era (ISSI), pp. 1–4 (2108)
14. Swai, P.S., Shandilya, V.K.: Gesture and speech recognition using Kinect device — a review. In: International Conference on Science and Technology for Sustainable Development, pp. 1–5 (2016)
15. Sholla, S., Naaz, R., Chishti, M.A.: Incorporating ethics in internet of things (IoT) enabled connected smart healthcare. In: IEEE/ACM International Conference on Connected Health: Applications, Systems and Engineering Technologies (CHASE), pp. 262–263 (2017)
16. Jangra, P., Gupta, M.: A design of real-time multilayered smart healthcare monitoring framework using IoT. In: International Conference on Intelligent and Advanced System (ICIAS), pp. 1–5 (2018)
17. Alabdulatif, A., Khalil, I., Yi, X., Guizani, M.: Secure edge of things for smart healthcare surveillance framework. IEEE Access 7, 31010–31021 (2019)
18. Saha, R., Kumar, G., Rai, M.K., Thomas, R., Lim, S.: privacy ensured e-healthcare for fog-enhanced IoT based applications. IEEE Access 7, 44536–44543 (2019)
19. Pathinarupothi, R.K., Durga, P., Rangan, E.S.: IoT-based smart edge for global health: remote monitoring with severity detection and alerts transmission. IEEE Internet Things J. 6(2), 2449–2462 (2019)
20. Tiangang, S., Zhou, L., Xiayang, D., Yi, W.: 3D Surface reconstruction based on Kinect sensor. Int. J. Comput. Theory Eng. 986–990 (2013)
21. Osunkoya, T., Chern, J.-C.: Gesture-based human-computer-interaction using Kinect for windows mouse control and powerpoint presentation. In: International Conference on Science and Technology for Sustainable Development, pp. 1–15 (2016)
22. Bartoli, L., Lassi, S.: Experimental study of results obtained from the interaction with softwares motion-based touchless created for habilitation-rehabilitation in users with diagnosis of autism spectrum disorders. Proc. Manuf. 3, Ahfe, 5176–5183 (2015)
23. Sheu, F.R., Chen, N.S.: Taking a signal: a review of gesturebased computing research in education. Comput. Educ. 78, 268–277 (2014)
24. Chang, Y., Chen, S., Huang, J.: Research in developmental disabilities a kinect-based system for physical rehabilitation: a pilot study for young adults with motor disabilities. Res. Dev. Disabil. 32(6), 2566–2570 (2011)
25. Gonçalves, N., Costa, S., Rodrigues, J., Soares, F.: Detection of stereotyped hand flapping movements in autistic children using the kinect sensor: a case study. In 2014 IEEE International Conference on Autonomous Robot Systems and Competitions, ICARSC, pp. 212–216 (2014)
26. Uzuegbunam, N., Wong, W., Cheung, S.S., Ruble, L.: Mebook : kinect-based self-modeling intervention for children with autism Department of Electrical & Computer Engineering and Department of Educational, School and Counseling Psychology University of Kentucky, Lexington KY, Multimed. Expo (ICME), 2015 IEEE Int. Conf., no. 1237134, (2015)
27. Malinverni, L., Mora-guiard, J., Padillo, V., Valero, L., Pares, N.: An inclusive design approach for developing video games for children with Autism Spectrum Disorder (2016)
28. H.J. Hsu: The potential of kinect as interactive educational technology. In: 2nd Int. Conf. Educ. Manag. Technol., 13, pp. 334–338 (2011)
29. Li, C., H.H.S. Ip.: AIMtechKinect: A kinect based interaction oriented gesture recognition system designed for students with severe intellectual disabilities. In: Proceedings - 13th International Conference on Computer-Aided Design and Computer Graphics, CAD/Graphics, pp. 322–329 (2013)

30. Roy, A.K., Soni, Y., Dubey, S.: Enhancing effectiveness of motor rehabilitation using kinect motion sensing technology. In: Global Humanitarian Technology Conference: South Asia Satellite (GHTC-SAS), IEEE, pp. 298–304 (2013)
31. Webster, D., Celik, O.: Systematic review of Kinect applications in elderly care and stroke rehabilitation. J. Neuroeng. Rehabil. **11**(1), 1–24 (2014)

CrawlBot: A Domain-Specific Pseudonymous Crawler

Vidyesh Shinde[1]([⊠]) [ID], Shahil Dhotre[1] [ID], Vedant Gavde[1] [ID], Ashwini Dalvi[2] [ID],
Faruk Kazi[1] [ID], and S. G. Bhirud[2] [ID]

[1] Department of Electronics Engineering, V.J.T.I. Mumbai, Mumbai, India
{vvshinde_b16,smdhotre_b16,vsgavde_b16,fskazi}@el.vjti.ac.in
[2] Department of Computer Engineering, V.J.T.I. Mumbai, Mumbai, India
{aadalvi_p19,sgbhirud}@ce.vjti.ac.in

Abstract. The Dark Net, a dark side of the internet, became a perfect hosting ground for criminal activities and services, including significant drug marketplaces, child and women sexual abuse, forged documents, homemade explosives, and likewise. The nature of the Dark Net makes it indifferent to searching through the indexed mechanism. Diverse approaches are suggested and attempted to gain useful insights from the Dark Net. In this paper, a focused crawling framework for uncovering material of child and women abuse that lies in the Surface and the Dark Net is proposed. A focused crawler is domain-specific and trained to selectively retrieve web pages that are related to a given domain from the Internet. One of the novel attributes of the crawler is traversing the Surface Net and the Dark Net in a pseudonymous way. During a single crawl session, it automatically selects hyperlinks, which are most likely to give related web pages and downloads pages that are relevant. The hyperlink selection method uses anchor text and local context of the hyperlink as a feature vector. Numerous web data mining and classification tasks utilize local contexts of hyperlinks. Focused or Topical crawlers have a major dependence on local contexts of hyperlinks. The relevancy of the page and hyperlinks is calculated using natural language processing and a sophisticated Artificial Neural Network (ANN) based classifier. The evaluation of the crawler indicates the high harvest rate and effectiveness of the crawler.

Keywords: TOR · Dark web crawling · ANN · Child sexual abuse material · Pseudonymous crawling · Hyperlink selection

1 Introduction

The history of the hidden web is almost as old as the history of the surface web. The same architecture and design that made the Surface Web possible, also makes the Dark Net possible. The Surface Web consists of web documents that search engines can find and then provide according to users' needs. As the tip of an iceberg is visible to us, a conventional web spider can see just a tiny fraction of the data that's available on the internet. The remaining part of the information which cannot be found on the regular search engines forms the Deep Net. It is gigantic, unlike the Surface Web. More

R. Agrawal et al. (Eds.): ICCEDE 2020, CCIS 1436, pp. 89–101, 2021.
https://doi.org/10.1007/978-3-030-84842-2_7

than 555 million domains have registered on the web and each contains multiple web pages. Many of these pages are not indexed and thus become part of the Deep Net. This enormous Deep Net has a small part known as the Dark Net. It is purposely hidden and is practically inaccessible via ordinary web browsers. The proper setup of the software and its configuration allows users to enter the Dark Net. It has gained popularity because it offers anonymity and facilitates secret communications. These significant features of the Dark Net attracted many cybercriminals to host illicit content and soon became a scary place to visit on the internet.

Child Sexual Abuse Material (CSAM) is content that portrays the sexual exploitation of children under the age of 18-years-old [1]. As a general term, CSAM belongs to child pornography as well as other forms of online child sexual offense. The usage of the Internet in CSAM crimes has caused substantial concern over the last decade, mainly as it links to the use of the Dark Net or content hosted on anonymized software services such as TOR [2]. Although the true prevalence of CSAM present on the Dark Net is unexplored, recent reports have revealed the popularity of child pornography sites among users of hidden services. A study of TOR conducted at the University of Portsmouth revealed that more than 83% of the Dark Net is created by visits to websites hosting child abuse material [3]. CSAM is different from other Dark Web-based illicit product marketplaces because only a tiny portion of CSAM is commercial. Surveys suggest only about 7.5% of CSAM on the Dark Net is sold for a profit. This is because the majority of CSAM functions as a barter system in which images are collected and traded within peer-to-peer (P2P) networks. The technological constraints required for accessing the elusive world of the Dark Net make crawling schemes employed for it more intricate, unlike the Surface Net.

Many organizations are working on this domain to prevent the online exploitation of children. 'Thorn' [4] is a non-profit body established in 2012 which focuses to protect children from sexual offense. One of its flagship products 'Spotlight' [5] was developed to enable law enforcement to collaborate beyond jurisdictions or national borders in identifying victims. Another initiative was taken by Thorn in this domain by the development of a tool called 'Safer' [6]. It provides companies with proper tools to eradicate CSAM from their platform.

The increasing number of content being uploaded on the web and technical complexities has made the manual investigation a very tedious task. Still, some websites like 'The Hidden wiki' and darknet search engines like Candle, Torch, etc. provide entry points to the Dark Net. The entry points gathered from these pages often lead to inactive websites and make the investigation futile. This paper highlights an effective tool that can be used by law enforcement and researchers to get the insight of the illicit content on the web. The proposed crawler can maneuver not only surface web but also the Dark Net to discover web resources on child and women abuse content. The crawler flawlessly follows related hyperlinks by adapting unique identities every time visiting a website. The next section talks about various works related to our crawler. Further, Sect. 2 discusses proposed architecture followed by pseudonymous and non-blocking crawling strategy, construction of feature vectors for the page classifier and link classifier. Section 4 displays the outcomes of the experiment for the CSAM domain and finally, Sect. 5 talks about the conclusion and future work.

2 Related Work

Several crawlers have developed to obtain the information from the Surface Net and the Hidden Web. Preliminary research has proposed various techniques and tools to obtain data from the visible web and the Hidden Net [7, 8]. Many studies describe the entry points of the Hidden Net [9, 10]. Generally, an exhaustive crawler and the focused crawler are employed in research areas. An Exhaustive or a Generic [11] crawler is the one that extracts information from the sites irrespective of its relevance to the domain and thus delays retrieval of domain-related information. Focused Crawler or Domain-specific crawler crawls topic or domain-related web pages and extracts information from it. ACHE crawler [12] can automatically search for information on a particular domain, producing a large number of relevant results from the web. We will now discuss a few crawlers related to our work.

Basic Exhaustive crawler proposed by Pant et al. [11] extracts all the information from the web without checking the relevancy of the data to the domain of interest. The basic flow of this type of crawler is to maintain the list of unvisited URLs called frontier. Initially, they consist of seed URLs provided by the users or another program. After this, the crawling loop starts by popping out one URL at a time from the frontier, visits that URL and extract all the information and hyperlinks present on the page and mark that page as visited so that the crawler won't encounter the same page again while crawling. This marking method helps for fast crawling process. Hyperlinks extracted from the page are added into the frontier, implemented as a FIFO queue because the crawler is working on the breadth-first algorithm. Now, if the crawler is ready to crawl another page, the next URL is popped out and the crawling process mentioned above continues till the termination. When the crawler reaches the depth (a certain number of pages have been crawled) or situation signals a dead-end (Frontier is empty-The crawler has no new page to fetch) the whole crawling process gets terminated.

ACHE crawler [12] is a domain-specific crawler developed at New York University. The darknet sites are generally not accessible by generic crawlers. The servers are located in the TOR network and require specific protocols for being accessed. ACHE uses external HTTP proxies such as Privoxy to crawl such sites. These proxies allow the crawler to route the request through the TOR network. It uses machine learning-based or regular expression based classifier to judge relevant and irrelevant web pages. It relies upon the title, body, and URL of the webpage as features for the classifier. The ACHE crawler employs the hard-focus and the soft-focus crawling strategy. In the hard-focus strategy, the crawler will discard all hyperlinks from irrelevant webpages. In the soft-focus strategy, it will discard hyperlinks only if the score calculated by the link classifier is lesser than the configured threshold value. It also uses a link classifier to determine the order of crawling. The link classifier assigns a score to the link based on its depth and discards links with depth higher than the predetermined threshold. ACHE uses a seed finder tool to collect a large set of seed URLs related to the chosen domain. The tool accepts a query from a user and redirects it to a search engine to obtain relevant seed URLs. It stores raw information and metadata of webpages as documents in the elasticsearch index.

The E-FFC (Enhanced Form-Focused Crawler) is a Deep Web Database (WDB) focused crawler proposed by Li et al. [13]. This crawler tries to tackle problems such as mining high-quality information from massive WDBs by automatically discovering and recognizing domain-specific entry points. It aims to overcome some common crawler deficiencies such as low stability of harvest and coverage rate. The crawler implements a two-step page classifier and link scoring to locate its target webpages by the breadth search strategy. E-FFC in its page classifier uses a page similarity threshold to check if a page belongs to a certain domain. The page similarity threshold is computed by extracting domain-specific pages from an available data set and comparing their domain feature vectors. The link classifier implemented in E-FFC considers a link scoring strategy with two features, immediate benefit link and delayed benefit link. Due to correlation among domains, the aforementioned methods also grab WDBs forms from other domains. To eliminate this, a generic (domain-independent) searchable form classifier and a domain-specific form classifier are introduced in a sequence in the E-FFC to filter domain-specific searchable forms. Further, to increase the rate of crawling, the E-FFC has adopted two types of link queues, single-level site link queue, and multi-level in-site link priority queues. As crawling stopping criteria, the E-FFC quits from a website after finding 4 forms in a crawling website or if the depth of visited pages away from its root page exceeds 5 levels.

The SmartCrawler proposed by Zhao et al. [7] is a two-stage domain-specific crawler framework that helps to locate hidden-web resources. The first stage is Site locating which uses a backlinks searching technique and site prioritization technique to find relevant links. The backlinks searching technique uses generic search engines to find the main pages of sites. These relevant links act as input to the next stage. The next stage is In-site exploring which utilizes 'balance link prioritizing' and 'form classifier'. This technique helps to harvest hidden web sources (such as searchable and non-searchable forms [13]) by covering a wide portion of the web as much as possible. It uses an adaptive learning technology that leverages data collected during past crawling session. This crawler has an effective harvesting rate for deep web interfaces or hidden web resources but is limited to the site hosted on the surface web.

Iliou et al. [8] proposed a focused crawling framework for extracting information on any given topic from the sites hosted on the Surface Net or the Dark Net (TOR, I2P, Freenet) [9]. They proposed 11 different hyperlink selection methods to find the most relevant sites on a given topic. The crawler uses a classifier-based approach to follow hyperlinks. They used Support Vector Machine (SVM) with RBF kernel classifier to calculate scores of hyperlinks. These methods are based on the dynamic linear combination of hyperlink and web page (parent and destination page) classification. Their results show high precision, recall, Surface Net hits, and Dark Net hits.

Different from the work mentioned above, our crawler CrawlBot is a domain-specific pseudonymous crawler for extracting relevant information and provides the insight of the surface web and Dark Net (TOR). Our crawler hides its identity by using randomly generated pseudo-user agents and IP rotation after every single crawl. It uses the link and the page classifier to collect relevant sources. This framework is bound to the CSAM domain. However, it can be easily reconfigured for any other domain.

3 Proposed Methodology

To crawl as many as relevant web pages and to collect data from them more efficiently, we have implemented a crawler framework that can cover the surface web as well as the Dark web. The detailed framework of the proposed crawler is illustrated in Fig. 1. The crawler automatically connects to the Surface Net or the Dark Net based on the link encountered. With the help of a pseudonymous crawling strategy, the crawler navigates the web uninterruptedly. It exploits the trained ANN model which forms the backbone of two main classifiers 1) link classifier, 2) page classifier. The page classifier is used in association with the link classifier to compute a relevancy score for a specific link. The crawler is implemented using Python 3.7 and Requests 2.2 library.

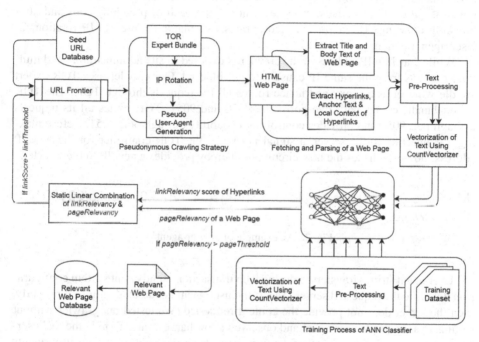

Fig. 1. The detailed framework of CrawlBot

First, seed URLs corresponding to the topic of interest are scraped from the search engine like Candle, Torch, etc. and inserted into the URL frontier. A URL is picked up from the frontier and before visiting the corresponding web page the crawler acquires a unique identity by changing user-agent and IP address. Then the web page is fetched and parsed to extract the title, body text, and hyperlinks. The extracted data is used by the page classifier to determine the relevancy score of the downloaded web page. If the score exceeds the threshold value then the corresponding web page is stored in the database. Further, the link classifier assigns relevancy score to each hyperlink considering anchor text and local context of hyperlink. Hyperlinks with a score greater than the predefined threshold are inserted in the frontier. While appending URLs to the frontier hyperlink with the highest score is appended first which ultimately increases the effectiveness of the crawler. In the coming part of this paper, a thorough explanation of each component of the proposed crawler is given.

3.1 Pseudonymous Crawling Strategy

Web crawlers are designed to retrieve data at a much faster pace and can dig deeper into the website than human beings. Multiple requests within a short period cause the server to overwhelm and reduce user experience. Thus, site administrators often employ anti-crawling mechanisms by finding crawling patterns such as a large number of requests from the same IP, usage of the old and same user-agent string. This hampers the overall performance of web crawlers. To tackle anti-crawling mechanisms and to increase the reach of our crawler, we have proposed a novel approach of pseudonymous and non-blocking crawling. The approach incorporates two major features 1) IP rotation, 2) User-agent rotation.

While crawling IP address of the crawler is exposed to site administrators and multiple requests from the same IP cause it to get blocked. Our crawler uses TOR expert bundle wrapper as a proxy and hence routes all the requests through TOR. The TOR expert bundle comes with two ports viz. 9050 and 9051. TOR routes all its requests through port 9050 and provides controlling capability through port 9051. Before making a connection to the server, a signal is sent to the TOR controller for the new IP address. It re-establishes the new circuit and thereby provides a new IP to the crawler.

Mozilla/5.0 (Windows NT 10.0; Win64; x64; rv:75.0) Gecko/20100101 Firefox/75.0

Fig. 2. An example of an user-agent

User-agent strings transferred during web transactions send client system configuration details to the requested server [14]. If the user-agent is outdated or not set properly, then the server does not provide the content requested. We tested our crawler without setting an appropriate user-agent and observed a low harvest rate. To hide the real user-agent of the crawler, it selects a fake user-agent from the pool of current user-agents before requesting a website. An example of a user-agent is shown in Fig. 2. This approach eventually provides multiple unique identities to our crawler and thus reduces the probability of getting blocked.

3.2 Page Classifier

During crawling our crawler comes across various kinds of web pages. The key is to cover a wide range of web pages related to the domain of interest while discarding irrelevant web pages and increase the overall harvest rate. This section describes the feature construction of a web page and classification mechanism.

After fetching, the page classifier classifies the web page as relevant or irrelevant. If the page is categorized as relevant, then it is marked as a flag and stored in a database. The downloaded web page is parsed and title and body content are extracted. Then extracted content is converted to lowercase, stemmed, tagged with part of speech followed by lemmatization and converted to vectors. The *CountVectorizer* is used to convert text into an encoded vector with the help of the learned vocabulary of a specific topic.

The feature space of feature vectors of the web page is given as:

$$FSP = \{T, B\} \tag{1}$$

where T, B are feature vectors corresponding to title and body text of the web page respectively. The resulting vector is fed to the ANN classifier which then decides if the page is relevant to the topic or not. The detailed process for page classification is described in Algorithm 1.

Algorithm 1: Page Classification

Input: Fetched HTML web page
Output: *pageRelevancy* score of web page
1 *page* = fetchPage()
2 *title, body* = extractTitleBody(*page*)
3 *pageText* = mergeText(*title, body*)
4 *processedText* = textPreprocessing(*pageText*)
5 *pageVector* = countVectorizer(*processedText*)
6 *pageRelevancy* = classifier(*pageVector*)

3.3 Link Classifier

In the context of CSAM, myriad web pages contain irrelevant hyperlinks which lead to pages which are the least interesting to Law Enforcement. This section sheds light upon the novel link selection approach combined with the page classifier, which selects links accurately.

The focused crawlers generally rely on the link context. topic-specific crawling works such as De Bra and Post [15] and Chakrabarti et al. [16]. applied the concept of link context in which the content of the entire page is treated as the context of the hyperlink embedded in it. SharkSearch [17] utilized the anchor text and some of the text in its neighborhood to determine the benefit of following the corresponding link. Iliou et al. [8] considered anchor text, terms within the URL and text window around the anchor text while calculating the relevancy of the hyperlink. Most of the sites encountered by our crawler are dark sites. Typically onion URLs contain automatically generated 16 (TOR version2) or 56 (TOR version3) character alpha-semi-numeric hashes which do not convey meaningful information. Hence crawler cannot rely on terms within the URLs and feature space of feature vector of the hyperlink is given as:

$$FSL = \{A, L\} \tag{2}$$

where A, L are feature vectors corresponding to anchor text and local context of the hyperlink respectively. This feature space is used by the link classifier to calculate *linkRelevancy*. This score is not sufficient to make a decision and thus the global context of the parent page is taken into consideration. Finally, *linkScore* of each hyperlink is calculated using a static linear combination of *linkRelevancy* and *pageRelevancy*. The score i.e. linkScore of each hyperlink is computed as:

$$linkScore = \alpha \times linkRelevancy + (1 - \alpha) \times pageRelevancy \qquad (3)$$

where α is the relative weight assigned to hyperlink relevancy score. The value of α plays an important role in selection of hyperlinks. Experimentally it is found that α = 0.6 yields satisfactory results. Then hyperlinks with *linkScore* greater than predefined *linkThreshold* are added to a queue. This queue is then sorted using *linkPrioritizing* and appended to URL frontier. The process of link classification is explained in Algorithm 2.

Algorithm 2: Link Classification

Input: Fetched HTML web page and *pageRelevancy* score
Output: *linkScore* of hyperlinks
1 *page* = fetchPage()
2 *relevantLinks* = createQueue()
3 *links* = extractLinks(*page*)
4 **for** *link in links* **do**
5   *anchorText* = extractAnchorText(*link*)
6   *anchorSocre* = classifier(*anchorText*)
7   *localContext* = extractLocalContext(*link*)
8   *locoScore* = classifier(*localContext*)
9   *linkRelevancy* = $0.5 \times anchorSocre + 0.5 \times locoScore$
       // Calculate static linear combination score using formula
         given in Eq.3
10   *linkScore* = statLinearCombination(*linkRelevancy, pageRelevancy*)
11   **if** *linkScore > linkThreshold* **then**
12   *relevantLinks*.add(*link*)

    // sort relevantLinks in ascending order according to linkScore
13 linkPrioritizing(*relevantLinks*)

The ANN-based classifier forms the fulcrum of CrawlBot, which helps in the page classifier as well as the link classifier. The classifier is trained on the pornography dataset. The dataset contains 46,719 positive samples and 54,968 negative samples. The dataset is parsed, its textual content is extracted, tokenization, stop words and punctuation removal, part of speech tagging and lemmatization is applied. The *CountVectorizer* weighing scheme is applied to convert textual data into feature vectors. Then, the classifier is trained using a fully-connected Artificial Neural Network. Since other domains, besides CSAM, might be of interest, the classifier can be easily re-trained on a new dataset related to the topic of interest. The next section provides the evaluation results for assessing the effectiveness of the proposed crawler.

4 Evaluation

4.1 Selection of a Classifier

The performance of various classifier approaches on 5-fold cross validation with *CountVectorizer* as a feature weighting scheme is depicted in the Table 1. The data for mentioned approaches is the same and the same text preprocessing is applied to data. The number of features is kept constant for all approaches to assess the performance of each approach.

Table 1. Performance of classification algorithms

Weighting scheme	Classifier	5-fold cross validation accuracy (in %)
CountVectorizer	Multinomial NB	95.18
CountVectorizer	SVM	95.58
CountVectorizer	ANN	96.51

The Multinomial Naive Bayes classifier is used to classify relevant and irrelevant web pages. It uses the multinomial distribution on the features. The classifier is tested using *CountVectorizer* weighting scheme. This approach is not suitable as accuracy is not desirable. Then SVM classifier was tested which improved the accuracy over the previous approach. Further, *CountVectorizer* with ANN classifier is trained and this approach boosted up the accuracy to 96.51%. Comparing the accuracy values, we got significant improvement with ANN + *CountVectorizer* compared to Multinomial Naive Bayes + *CountVectorizer*. This shows the efficiency of the chosen classifier in the categorization task.

4.2 Nature of Darknet and It's Interconnectivity

The experiments carried out for a different number of web pages shows that the Dark Net and the Surface Net are interconnected for the CSAM domain. Table 2 represents the number of surface web links found while crawling the Dark Net. These results prove that several darknet links contain hyperlinks directed to surface web sites. The proposed crawler does not get obstructed by this interconnectivity and seamlessly crawls the Dark Net as well as the surface web during a single crawl session.

Another experiment conducted to monitor the nature of the Dark Net. The pro-posed crawler was run for ten consecutive days on the same set of the Dark Net links. The graph shown in Fig. 3 represents a very unstable nature of the Dark Net. The Dark Net links also known as the hidden services often go offline and recuperate under a new domain name [18]. Hence it is very important to acquire data of every new hidden service as soon as it appears to analyze its online activity. TOR Hidden Services related to CSAM captured by our crawler are given in Table 3. It shows the format of links of the Dark Net.

Table 2. Interconnectivity of the Dark Net and the Surface Net

Pages crawled	Links found	Surface net links	Dark net links
100	844	104	740
200	1391	112	1279
300	1858	123	1735
500	2048	125	1923

Table 3. Snapshot of crawled links

Onion links	Topic
z4c4kdaf42gem4x3fksjjan7ecjfqt5zchoa7xpi7ujfiu2jqrzphqad.onion	Women abuse
s3icn6jrwkjov4pknz3iilcbuy7ahgeu7af7gqd7bjkf7gywbj44weid.onion	Pedophile
videocp3e3d65efnafl5jt3kqcavav755e7o7dvbncjynsmxhlrwpyad.onion	Pedophile
nkmxbnup44toysy5na7zqoq2bomuwt34akapfp62lbscdptaiim7void.onion	CSAM

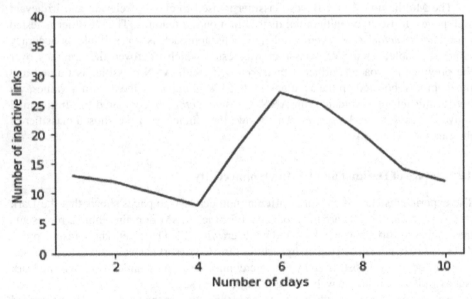

Fig. 3. Unstable nature of the dark web

4.3 Harvest Rate

This section presents the findings of experiments carried out to determine the link harvesting capability of the crawler. Many web pages contain hyperlinks that do not always point to related web pages and often misguide the crawler. The value of *linkThreshold* plays the main role in selecting relevant links efficiently. To explain this, Table 4 provides the number of relevant and irrelevant links found by the crawler. The experiment was conducted by changing the value of *linkThreshold* while keeping the number of crawled pages to 200. The link-Threshold value 0.4 appears to be effective in properly distinguishing between related and non-related links. Hence it is obvious that the usage of the page classifier in combination with the link classifier and proper choice of *linkThreshold* improves the total effectiveness of the crawler.

Table 4. Effectiveness of crawler in link harvesting

Values of *linkThreshold*	Relevant links	Irrelevant links	Total links
0.4	768	623	1391
0.5	723	668	1391
0.6	682	709	1391
0.7	659	732	1391
0.8	627	764	1391

The performance of the focused crawler is generally measured by the harvest rate. It determines the fraction of the crawled web pages that are relevant to a given topic. To judge whether a given web page is related to a given topic or not, the crawler relies on the classifier. As discussed previously, the ANN-based classifier performs well with the *CountVectorizer* weighting scheme. We carried out three crawling sessions with different values of *pageThreshold* designated as 't' in Fig. 4(a). The value of α is set to 0.4 and the crawler was allowed to crawl 50 pages and the harvest rate of each session was recorded. The Harvest Rate is computed as:

$$HarvestRate = \frac{1}{N} \sum_{n=i}^{N} PageRelevancy_i \qquad (4)$$

where N is the number of pages crawled and the *pageRelevancy* is a binary score of a web page. As discussed in Sect. 3.3, the overall link Score of a hyperlink depends upon the value of α. The proper choice of α ultimately determines the overall link harvest rate of the crawler. The different values of link harvest rate were recorded by changing α value. This experiment was conducted by setting *linkThreshold* value to 0.4 and results are depicted in Fig. 4(b). The link harvest rate is a fraction of links found by the crawler which are relevant to a topic. The Harvest Rate for link is calculated as:

$$HarvestRatelink = \frac{1}{N} \sum_{n=i}^{N} LinkScore_i \qquad (5)$$

where N is the number of links found during crawling and the *linkScore* is a binary score of a hyperlink. It is obvious from the graph shown in Fig. 4(b) that the value of $\alpha = 0.6$ improves the harvest rate of links. Additionally, links collected by the crawler when manually investigated revealed that the values 0.7 and 0.8 gives some fraction of off-topic links.

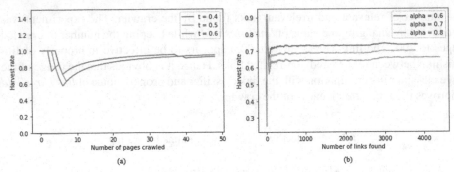

Fig. 4. (a) The comparison of harvest rate for different values of t, (b) The comparison of link harvest rate for different values of alpha

5   Conclusion and Future Work

This work proposed a web crawler framework capable of seamlessly crawling the Surface Net as well as the Dark Net (predominantly TOR) within a single crawl. It employed a method wherein the crawler can automatically connect to the Surface Net or the Dark Net, based on the type of link it encounters. With the help of a pseudonymous crawling strategy, the crawler can navigate the web uninterruptedly. The crawler utilized the trained ANN model which formed the foundation of both the link classifier and the page classifier. The page classifier in association with the link classifier helped to compute a relevancy score for a specific link. The evaluation results showed the effectiveness of the crawler and also how ANN-based classifier is superior over other classification approaches.

The proposed crawler can be employed by government bodies to track malicious content on the internet, gather specific types of information from websites and analyse social media, blogs and forum data for illicit material such as drugs, child pornography, and human trafficking. The crawler can be easily re-trained to explore other domains of the Dark Web as well.

Particularly, in the CSAM domain, many pages contain many images and thus crawler fails to classify the web page accurately. This bottleneck of the crawler will be eliminated in the future work with the incorporation of Image Classification which will greatly enhance the performance of the crawler which is currently developed to extract the content and determine its relevance using Text Classifier. The crawler can also be made more robust for crawling other dark web sites such as I2P and FreeNet.

Acknowledgement. The authors are very grateful to the Center of Excellence in Complex and Nonlinear Dynamical Systems (COE-CNDS) under TEQIP-III funding for providing the infrastructure necessary to develop the crawler. We would also like to thank the members of the lab for their worthy feedback and comments.

References

1. Liggett, R.: Commercial child sexual abuse markets on the dark web. White Paper. School of Criminal Justice, Michigan State University.
2. McCoy, D., Bauer, K., Grunwald, D., Kohno, T., Sicker, D.: Shining light in dark places: Understanding the Tor network. In: Borisov, N., Goldberg, I. (Eds.) Privacy Enhancing Technologies. PETS 2008. Lecture Notes in Computer Science, vol. 5134. Springer, Berlin, Heidelberg. https://doi.org/10.1007/978-3-540-70630-45 (2008)
3. Finklea, K.: Dark Web. Congressional Research Service (2017)
4. Thorn: https://www.thorn.org
5. Spotlight: https://www.thorn.org/spotlight/
6. Safer: https://getsafer.io/about-safer/
7. Zhao, F., Zhou, J., Nie, C., Huang, H., Jin, H.: SmartCrawler: a two-stage crawler for efficiently harvesting deep-web interfaces. In: IEEE Transactions on Services Computing, vol. 9, no. 4, pp. 608–620, IEEE. https://doi.org/10.1109/TSC.2015.2414931 (2016)
8. Iliou, C., Kalpakis, G., Tsikrika, T., Vrochidis, S., Kompatsiaris, I.: Hybrid focused crawling on the surface and the dark web. EURASIP J. Inf. Secur. 2017(1), 1–13 (2017). https://doi.org/10.1186/s13635-017-0064-5
9. Ali, A., et al.: TOR vs I2P: a comparative study. In: 2016 IEEE International Conference on Industrial Technology (ICIT), pp. 1748–1751. IEEE, Taipei. https://doi.org/10.1109/ICIT.2016.7475027 (2016)
10. Mani, A., Wilson-Brown, T., Jansen, R., Johnson, A., Sherr, M.: Understanding Tor usage with privacy-preserving measurement. In: IMC 2018: Proceedings of the Internet Measurement Conference 2018, pp. 175–187. ACM, New York. https://doi.org/10.1145/3278532.3278549 (2018)
11. Pant, G., Srinivasan, P., Menczer, F.: Crawling the web. In: Web Dynamics. Springer, Berlin (2004)
12. ACHE Crawler Documentation, Release latest. New York University (April 2019)
13. Li, Y., Wang, Y., Du, J.: E-FFC: an enhanced form-focused crawler for domain-specific deep web databases. J. Intell. Inform. Syst. 40, 159–184 (2013)
14. Kline, J., Cahn, A., Barford, P., Sommers, J.: On the structure and characteristics of user agent string. In: IMC 2017: Proceedings of the 2017 Internet Measurement Conference, pp. 184–190. ACM, New York. https://doi.org/10.1145/3131365.3131406 (2017)
15. De Bra, P., Post, R.D.J.: Information retrieval in the world-wide web: making client-based searching feasible. Comput. Netw. ISDN Syst. 27(2), 183–192 (1994)
16. Chakrabarti, S., van den Berg, M., Dom, B.: Focused crawling: a new approach to topic-specific web resource discovery. Comput. Netw. 31(11–16), 1623–1640 (1999). https://doi.org/10.1016/S1389-1286(99)00052-3
17. Hersovici, M., Jacovi, M., Maarek, Y., Pelleg, D., Shtalhaim, M., Ur, S.: The shark-search algorithm. An application: tailored Web site mapping. Comput. Netw. ISDN Syst. 30(1–7), 317–326 (1998). https://doi.org/10.1016/S0169-7552(98)00038-5
18. Chertoff, M., Simon, T.: The impact of the dark web on internet governance and cyber security. In: Global Commission on Internet Governance Paper Series: No. 6 (2015)

A Lightweight Authentication and Key Establishment Scheme for Smart Metering Infrastructure

Jaya Singh[✉] [iD], Yuvaraj Rajendra[iD], Venkatesan Subramanian[iD],
and Om Prakash Vyas[iD]

Department of Information Technology, Indian Institute of Information Technology,
Allahabad, India
{pcl2016003,venkat,opvyas}@iiita.ac.in

Abstract. The smart metering infrastructure of the smart grid needs an efficient security mechanism since the smart meters have limited computational power and storage. Considering the limitation, this paper presents a lightweight au-thentication and key establishment scheme to use between the Neighbourhood Area Network (NAN) gateway and domestic smart meter. The scheme includes one-time registration of smart meter with NAN gateway and multiple times mutual authentication between the NAN gateway and smart meter. The proposed protocol ensured security with minimum computation and storage to enable limited power smart meter to authenticate itself with NAN. The security robustness of the proposed model was analysed and proved using the Automated Validation of Internet Security Protocols and Applications (AVISPA) tool. Also, the performance evaluation shows the effectiveness of the proposed scheme with the property of efficiency and lightweight than the existing schemes with respect to the computational cost.

Keywords: Security · Authentication · Key establishment · Smart grid · Smart metering

1 Introduction

In the present time, Internet of Things (IoT) devices are mounting rapidly. According to a report by Gartner and Cisco [1,2], this epidemic growth will reach 25 to 50 billions respectively in this year. With this exponential ascent in the number of devices, the IoT is preparing to proceed on edge computing for serving low latency and high bandwidth with better connectivity. The concept of smart grid and smart metering has got great concentration recently. The recent progress in the Information and Communication Technologies (ICT) has promoted the Smart Grid (SG) as essential part of IoT services. The SG has emerged in IoT as the future of energy industry and power system with the advantages of fast computing, sensing, monitoring and balancing energy load,

© Springer Nature Switzerland AG 2021
R. Agrawal et al. (Eds.): ICCEDE 2020, CCIS 1436, pp. 102–114, 2021.
https://doi.org/10.1007/978-3-030-84842-2_8

supplying uninterrupted energy, adequate power quality and efficient communication technique to properly manage the network of electricity [3,4]. While improving efficiency, reliability, energy supply quality and flexibility [5], SGs suffers from high latency and low QoS [6] and different attacks as they are depend on ICT [7]. The authentication and secure key establishment scheme are the base security factor to overcome various attacks. The mutual authentication and key exchange provides the secure communication by ensuring trust identity among the users communicating through public network without exchanging any susceptible knowledge publicly [8]. There are many traditional protocols based on public key which are doubtful and inappropriate for smart metering infrastructure since most of the devices in the smart grid or lightweight IoT devices and dependency on a Certification Authority (CA) for issuing certificate repeatedly.

Hence, it is extensive to construct a valuable and lightweight security solution for smart grid especially for the smart metering infrastructure since the light node smart meters does not have sufficient computational and storage power. Considering these factors, we are proposing a lightweight authentication and key establishment protocol for SG Infrastructure. The lightweight and robust mutual authentication, secure session key generation and exchange in the smart metering infrastructure of the smart grid resists different attacks thus result in providing reliable, uninterrupted and efficient power supply.

The remainder of this paper is arranged as follows: Sect. 2 presents the related work of the scheme and our contribution to this paper while Sect. 3 presents the system model and assumptions. Section 4 presents the proposed scheme and proof of correctness while theoretical security analysis is provided in Sect. 5. The computational cost analysis of the proposed scheme and its comparison with other schemes is presented in Sect. 6 and Sect. 7 concludes the paper and provides future work directions.

2 Related Work

A number of authentication and key establishment protocols have been presented to deal with the security related concerns in SG Infrastructure in recent year [9–16]. An anonymous authentication key distribution scheme with encryption and ID-based signature was proved by Tsai and Lo [17]. Compared to this scheme, He et al. [18] presented a new protocol with less computation cost but it was found vulnerable to temporary secret key leakage. A spatial data aggregation protocol with lightweight cryptography was presented by Gope and Sikdar [19]. A three- factor authentication protocol with traditional anonymity for smart meter was presented by Wazid et al. [20] but this protocol does not support dynamic revocation to remove malicious smart meters.

A lightweight authentication and key agreement protocol proposed by Kumar et al. [21] that achieves identity anonymity using symmetric encryption, but in this scheme all smart meters are registered by the NAN gateway hence NAN gateway has to preserve a lot of symmetric keys for numerous smart meters. Mahmood et al. [22] presented a high efficient authentication protocol but it does not support anonymity. So, Mahmood et al. [23] presented other anonymous key management scheme for SG, but [24] argue that this protocol fails to provide mutual authentication.

In 2019, Garg et al. [25] presented a lightweight authentication scheme, but this protocol does not support anonymity as smart meters sends their real Identity ($I(sm)$) to the NAN gateway for communication request. An efficient and anonymous identity based authentication scheme for MEC was proposed by Jia et al. [26] but they did not consider key management for communicating users. An authentication and key management strategy for edge-cloud computing was presented by Kahvazadeh et al. [27] that authenticate all the devices through control area unit (CAU) whic is supposed to be a trusted entity but this protocol does not support anonymity and so not suitable for SGs. Some protocol was presented based on ring signature [28], blind signature [29] and group signature [30], but it is known that these signature schemes are time consuming and suffers from different drawbacks as discussed earlier.

More recently, J Wang et al. [24] proposed an anonymous authentication scheme based on blockchain for edge based SG systems that make use of smart contract to verify the real identity securely using Registration Authority (RA), but smart contracts also suffers from the issue of transaction processing speed and scalability problem in blockchain. They are also highly dependent on programmers and vulnerable to bugs. Hence, it is a big challenge to design an improved and efficient lightweight authentication and key establishment scheme with less complexity, latency and communication cost with high scalability for smart metering infrastructure.

2.1   Contribution

The contributions of this paper to provide secure smart metering infrastructure for the smart grid are as follows:

1. Proposed a lightweight and efficient authentication and key establishment protocol that supports dynamic key exchange and secure communication.
2. The security strength of the proposed model is analysed using Automated Verification of Internet Security Protocol and Application (AVISPA) [31].
3. The security analysis and computational cost measurement proves that the proposed scheme is also deployable in real time smart metering infrastructure.

3   System Model

This section presents the systematic model of the proposed scheme with some assumptions.

3.1   Entities

The smart metering infrastructure of the proposed scheme consist of the following three entities:

1. **Registration Authority (RA):** The registration authority is a centralized entity or service provider trusted by each of the members in the smart metering infrastructure. The RA is also responsible for generate and distribute the key materials (Public and Private key pairs) to all the members participating in SG service utilization.
2. **Smart Meter (SM):** The smart meters are usually installed at Home area network(HAN) and accountable for maintaining the energy consumption details of the consumer. These energy consumption data values are sent to the RA through NAN gateway. The SMs are generally connected to the nearest NAN gateway.
3. **Neighbour Area Network (NAN) gateway:** The Neighbour area network (NAN) gateway are also perform as edge server that work as intermediary node or utility controller between RA and SMs for providing electricity services to its nearby SMs and send their usage report to the RA.

3.2 Assumptions

Furthermore, the list of assumption adopted in this scheme are as follows:

- The public keys of all entities are known to all and the identities of NAN are known to SMs as in smart metering infrastructure, NAN gateways are present as broadcast nodes since providing services on time and demand, so there is not any requirement for identity anonymity for NAN gateways.
- The clocks are synchronized for SMs and NANs.
- The RA is connected to the NAN and SM in a secure manner. Although, the communication between NAN and SMs are public and not secure so, the proposed scheme is designed for authenticating and key exchanging to ensure security between these two entities.

3.3 Security Requirements

The security requirements that must be satisfied in a practical authentication and key establishment scheme of smart metering infrastructure are as follows:

1. Mutual Authentication: The mutual authentication of the SMs and NANs are required to permit only the registered entities of smart metering infrastructure to communicate. The nodes mutually verify their identity before sending messages.
2. No Online RA: To solve the issue of single point failure and minimizing communication overhead, it is required to achieve mutual authentication between the entities without involving RA every time.
3. Session Key Agreement: During the proposed scheme's execution, a similar session key should be generated on both side for further message exchange and it should not be disclosed to any other entity including RA.
4. Confidentiality: Only the authorized entities able to interpret the communication messages.

5. Identity Anonymity: The identity privacy is necessary for the SMs so that attacker can never get the real identity of the SM while authentication phase.
6. Flexible against other Attacks: To improve the smart metering infrastructure security, the proposed scheme is required to provide elasticity against different common attacks.

4   Proposed Protocol

The challenge of this algorithm is to perform efficiently by providing resiliency, low latency, high security and scalability to ensure the best performance.

4.1   Initial Phase

This phase is performed by RA in the starting of implementation of the system. The proposed scheme uses the Elliptic Curve Cryptography (ECC) with the Secure Hash Algorithm (SHA) respectively for encryption and one way hashing. A cyclic additive group $\mathbb{G}$ choosen by RA with the prime order n and a generator P on an Elliptic curve E over a finite field $\mathbb{F}_p$. Then RA takes a psudorandom number $d_T \in \mathbb{Z}_q^*$ as its master private key, calculates corresponding public key $Q_T = d_T \cdot P$ and selects a secure one way hash function $h()$. Now RA keeps d_T secret and publish the other parameters $(\mathbb{G}, P, n, Q_T, h())$.

4.2   Registration Phase

This phase is executed between RA and SM/NAN gateway when a new SM or NAN gateway joins the smart metering infrastructure. The Registration phase computation and communication is shown in Fig. 1. Initially, the SM_i sends its identity ID_i to the RA for registration. The RA firstly checks whether this SM has registered previously or not, if yes, then terminate the request, otherwise calculates key material for SM_i by selecting a random number $r_i \in \mathbb{Z}*_q$ and calculate $R_i = r_i \cdot P$. Now, it calculate the $EID_i = h(ID_i\|R_i)$ and the secret key for SM_i as $d_A = r_i + d_T \cdot EID_i$ and its corresponding public key $Q_A = d_A \cdot P$.

Now RA sends (EID_i, d_A, Q_A, R_i) to the SM_i via a secret channel. The secret channel is established using the public key of smart meter and it is used only once afterwards RA generated key will be used. After getting these key materials from RA, SM_i just verifies the validity of $d_A \cdot P = R_i + Q_T \cdot EID_i$ and $EID_i = h(ID_i\|R_i)$ and then stores d_A and EID_i securely after verifying them successfully.

In same way, NAN_j also register with RA by sending its ID_j to RA and gets back its key materials EID_j, R_j, d_N and Q_N from RA via secret message and store them after successfully verification.

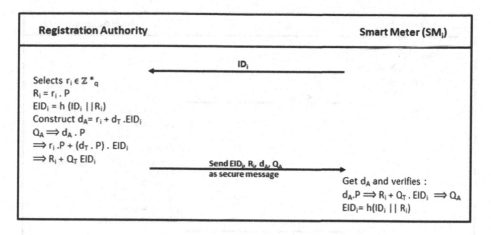

Fig. 1. Registration phase of our protocol

4.3 Authentication Phase

The process of the authentication between smart meter and NAN gateway is shown in Fig. 2. This phase is initiated by the smart meter whenever it needs to communicate with NAN gateway. The smart meter SM_i use the key materials received from RA, choose a random number $a \in \mathbb{Z}*_q$ and calculates $A = a \cdot P$ and $A' = a \cdot Q_N$. Then it computes $K_A = A' \oplus EID_i \oplus T_i$, where T_i is the current timestamp. Now it start communication with its closer NAN gateway NAN_j by sending $< A, R_i, K_A, T_i >$ through public channel.

The NAN gateway NAN_j receives these parameters from SM SM_i and firstly verifies if $|T_i - T_i'| \leq \triangle T$ where $\triangle T$ is the predefined threshold value and T_i' is the current timestamp. Then it verifies $A' = A \cdot d_N$ and extract $EID_i' = A' \oplus K_A \oplus T_i$ and construct $Q_A' = R_i + Q_T \cdot EID_i'$ and checks whether $Q_A' \stackrel{?}{=} Q_A$ (the public key of SM SM_i). If they both are equal then verified and accepted, otherwise terminate the session by NAN_j. Now NAN_j selects a random integer b and calculates $B = b \cdot P$, $B' = b \cdot Q_A$ and $Z = b \cdot A$. Then it calculates session key of NAN gateway $SK_N = h(A||B||Z||T_j)$, where T_j is the timestamp of NAN_j. Finally it sends $< B, R_j, K_N, T_j >$ to SM_i.

On receiving this message from NAN_j, SM_i first verifies the $T_j - T_j' \leq \triangle T$ and $B' = B \cdot d_A$. It then extract $EID_j' = B' \oplus K_N \oplus T_j$, construct $Q_N' = R_j + Q_T \cdot EID_j'$ and checks whether $Q_N' \stackrel{?}{=} Q_N$ (the public key of NAN NAN_j). If SM_i find both are equal then received parameters are accepted otherwise terminates the ongoing handshake to establish the mutual authentication and secure channel. After verifying, SM_i calculates $Y = a \cdot B$, Session key of smart meter $SK_A = h(B||A||Y||T_i)$ and communicate further through this session key.

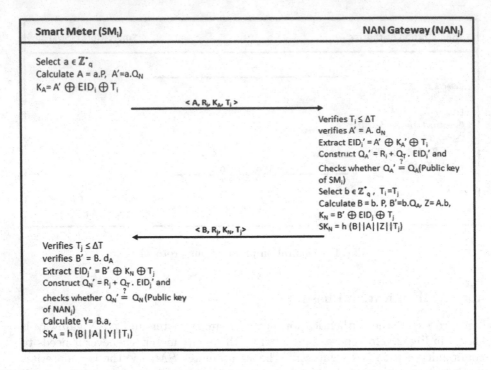

Fig. 2. Authentication and key agreement phase of our scheme

4.4 Proof of Correctness

In this section, we provide the proof of correctness of the proposed protocol. In the Fig. 2, the verification of A' is as follows:

$$A' = a \cdot Q_N \longrightarrow a \cdot d_N \cdot P \longrightarrow a \cdot P \cdot d_N = A \cdot d_N \qquad (1)$$

Thus, A' get verified at NAN side. Similarly SM also verifies B' received from NAN gateway. The correctness of $Q'_A \stackrel{?}{=} Q_A$ is as follows:

$$Q'_A = R_i + Q_T \cdot EID'_i \longrightarrow r_i \cdot P + d_T \cdot P \cdot EID'_i \longrightarrow (r_i + d_T \cdot EID'_i) \cdot P \longrightarrow d_A \cdot P = Q_A \quad (2)$$

Therefore, $Q'_A = Q_A$.

In the Fig. 2, we get the value of Y at SM and Z at NAN gateway but both are equal. On deriving from Y, we get $Y = Z$:

$$Y = a \cdot B \longrightarrow a \cdot b \cdot P \longrightarrow a \cdot P \cdot b \longrightarrow A \cdot b = Z \qquad (3)$$

hence, $SK_A = SK_N$.

Table 1. Comparison of security properties supported by different schemes

Property	Kumar et al. [21]	Garg et al. [25]	Wang et al [24]	Proposed
Mutual authentication	Y	Y	Y	Y
Session key agreement	Y	Y	Y	Y
No online RA	-	Y	Y	Y
Pseudo-anonymity	Y	Weak	Y	Y
Un-traceability	-	-	Y	Y
Forward secrecy	Y	Y	Y	Y
Resist replay attack	Y	Y	Y	Y
Resist impersonation attack	Y	Y	Y	Y
Resist stolen verifier attack	-	-	Y	Y
Mitigation of DoS attack	Y	Y	-	Y
Resist MITM attack	Y	Y	Y	Y

Y - Satisfies the security property, - Not discussed

5   Security Analysis

This section will provide the details of security analysis supported by this system. The Table 1 shows the comparisons of our protocol with other sechems to understand it better.

1. **Support Mutual Authentication:** The proposed scheme supports mutual authentication as we have shown in the previous section. The entities SM_i and NAN_j authenticate each other by verifying timestamps, A', B' and constructing Q'_A and Q'_N which are constructed by the respective communicating entities. This verification can not be possible without their respective secret keys d_A and d_N.

2. **Session key Agreement:** To get the accurate session key, an attacker needs the values of a or b which is not possible to get because these values are not shared via public channel and secret to their respective generator. The calculation of a and b from A and B is elliptic curve discrete log problem (ECDLP).

3. **No Online RA:** It is clear from the scheme that it does not need to call RA during the authentication phase and for further communication.

4. **Support Pseudo-Anonymity:** The proposed scheme supports privacy of SMs by providing identity anonymity. The original identity ID of smart meter is shared only at the registration phase not in the iterative authentication phase and further communication.

5. **Resists Traceablility:** This authentication scheme supports identity anonymity and unlinkability for SM, so the behaviour of the SM can not be traced by any outside attacker.

6. **Forward Secrecy:** A perfect forward secrecy involve the session keys that should never be compromised even if the private keys of entities and messages are compromised. In this scheme attacker cannot get the values of a and b to calculate A and B because a and b are randomly chosen by the entities and not sent via public channel.

7. **Oppose Replay attacks:** Proposed scheme is resist against replay attack as it uses timestamps with all messages exchanges.
8. **Resilience against Impersonation Attacks:** This proposed scheme also resist impersonation attacks since the messages shared via public channels are computed through their respective private keys.
9. **Resist Stolen Verifier Attacks:** The stolen verifier attack is not possible in this scheme as the RA keeps only the ID and their respective EID in its storage and removes the Key material of that particular entity after sharing with the entities.
10. **Mitigation of Denial of Service:** The proposed protocol mitigates DoS attack since the messages coming from an entity is firstly validated according to timestamp and random number multiplier (example $A'' = d_N \cdot A$).
11. **Resist Man-in-the-Middle (MITM) Attack:** The MITM attack is not possible in this scheme as the messages are calculating through the random number and private keys of respective entities and an attacker can not get both of them since those are not transmitted via public channel.

5.1 Formal Security Analysis

The formal security analysis of this proposed scheme has done by Automated Verification of Internet Security Protocols and Applications (AVISPA) tool [31] which is well noted in the academia [12,14,21]. AVISPA is a suite of application that helps in validating the internet security protocols in some automated manner.

It consist of four particular model-controllers for checking: on the fly model-checker; SAT-based model checker; constraint logic based attack searcher; tree automata based on automatic approx. of analysis of security schemes. AVISPA scripting language is known as High level protocol specification language (HLPSL) which is a role based language, so it recognize the members as operator performing different duty and accountability in complete protocol. This is presented as the transaction. The obtained result from AVISPA is presented in Fig. 3 and it shows that the proposed mutual authentication and the key establishment scheme is safe against on the fly model-checker (OFMC) and constraint logic based attack searcher back ends and executes within a bounded number of sessions. Hence the proposed scheme is safe against the attacks.

6 Computational Cost Analysis

In this section, we present the performance of our protocol compared with two recent related schemes Garg et al. [25] and Wang et al. [24]. The Table 2 shows that our scheme provides mutual authentication and key establishment with minimum number of cryptographic operations as compared with existing schemes. The T_m refers ECC point-multiplication, T_h refers one-way hash function and T_a refers point addition. Although Garg et al. [25] have shown $2T_m$ in SM and $2T_m$ in NAN, but according to our calculation we have considered $4T_m$s on each

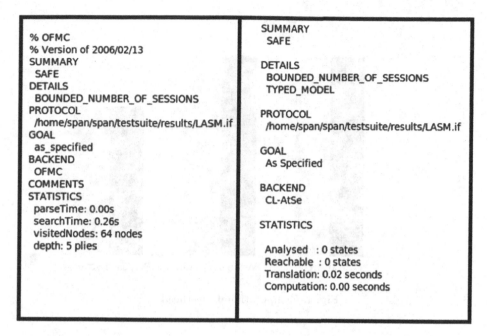

Fig. 3. Formal security verification of designed protocol on AVISPA

Table 2. Comparison of different schemes with respect to number of cryptographic operations

Scheme	Smart Motor	NAN Gateway	Total
Garg et al. [25]	$4T_m + 4T_h$	$4T_m + 4T_h$	$8T_m + 8T_h$
Wang et al. [24]	$4T_m + 1T_a + 5T_h$	$4T_m + 1T_a + 6T_h$	$8T_m + 2T_a + 11T_h$
Proposed	$3T_m + 1T_h$	$3T_m + 1T_h$	$6T_m + 2T_h$

entity. The total computation overhead of our proposed protocol is $6T_m + 2T_h$, which is lower than both the existing schemes.

To show the computational advantage of the proposed scheme, We have considered the computational time of various cryptographic operations presented in the Kumar et al. [21] scheme and compared with existing works. The execution time of ECC point multiplication (T_m) is 2900 ms and one-way hash (T_h) is 39 ms. The Fig. 4 shows the comparison of computation overhead of different schemes of the smart metering infrastructure including the SM and NAN gateway cryptographic operations. The total computation overhead of our proposed protocol is $6T_m + 2T_h = 6(2900) + 2(39) = 17478$ ms however computation overhead of Garg et al. [25] is 23512 ms and Wang et al. [24] has 23590 excluding the point addition (T_a). Hence our proposed scheme has less overhead when compared with the existing schemes.

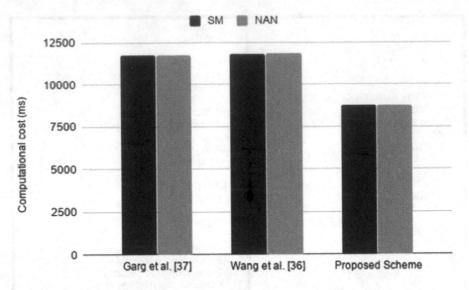

Fig. 4. Computational Overhead

It is clear from the Table 2 and Fig. 4 that our proposed schemes takes less computation cost at both levels with respect to the number of cryptographic operations when compared with existing schemes. Hence the proposed scheme is suitable for the light smart meter of the smart metering infrastructure.

7   Conclusion

The security is very essential while smart meter and the NAN communicates in the smart metering infrastructure. To ensure the mutual authentication and security, we present a lightweight authentication and key establishment scheme. The proposed scheme uses the Elliptic Curve Cryptography and one way hash function to provide a secure mutual authentication and symmetric key establishment among the entities. The security analysis and evaluation shows that this scheme is secure against several attacks and malicious activities. In addition, the formal analysis done on the AVISPA tool demonstrate the proposed scheme's safety and security against different threat models. The computational cost analysis proved that the proposed scheme needs less overhead when compared with the existing schemes. The future work of this paper is to overcome the insider attack.

References

1. Corsaro A.: Cloudy, foggy and misty internet of things. In: Proceedings of the 7th ACM/SPEC on International Conference on Performance Engineering (2016)
2. Brody P, Pureswaran V. Device democracy: Saving the future of the internet of things. IBM, September (2014)
3. Saxena, N., Choi, B.J.: State of the art authentication, access control, and secure integration in smart grid. Energies 8(10), 11883–11915 (2015)
4. Chaudhary, R., Aujla, G.S., Garg, S., Kumar, N., Rodrigues, J.J.: SDN-enabled multi-attribute-based secure communication for smart grid in IIoT environment. IEEE Trans. Ind. Inform. 14(6), 2629–2640 (2018)
5. Lyu, L., Nandakumar, K., Rubinstein, B., Jin, J., Bedo, J., Palaniswami, M.: PPFA: privacy preserving fog-enabled aggregation in smart grid. IEEE Trans. Ind. Inform. 14(8), 3733–3744 (2018)
6. Kaur, K., Garg, S., Aujla, G.S., Kumar, N., Rodrigues, J.J., Guizani, M.: Edge computing in the industrial internet of things environment: software-defined-networks-based edge-cloud interplay. IEEE Commun. Mag. 56(2), 44–51 (2018)
7. Kumar, N., Kaur, K., Misra, S.C., Iqbal, R.: An intelligent RFID-enabled authentication scheme for healthcare applications in vehicular mobile cloud. Peer-to-Peer Netw. Appl. 9(5), 824–840 (2016)
8. Wu, L., Wang, J., Choo, K.K.R., He, D.: Secure key agreement and key protection for mobile device user authentication. IEEE Trans. Inf. Foren. Secur. 14(2), 319–330 (2018)
9. Fouda, M.M., Fadlullah, Z.M., Kato, N., Lu, R., Shen, X.S.: A lightweight message authentication scheme for smart grid communications. IEEE Trans. Smart Grid 2(4), 675–685 (2011)
10. Chim, T.W., Yiu, S.M., Li, V.O., Hui, L.C., Zhong, J.: PRGA: privacy-preserving recording & gateway-assisted authentication of power usage information for smart grid. IEEE Trans. Depend. Secur. Comput. 12(1), 85–97 (2014)
11. Li, H., Lu, R., Zhou, L., Yang, B., Shen, X.: An efficient merkle-tree-based authentication scheme for smart grid. IEEE Sys. J. 8(2), 655–663 (2013)
12. Nicanfar, H., Jokar, P., Beznosov, K., Leung, V.C.: Efficient authentication and key management mechanisms for smart grid communications. IEEE Syst. j. 8(2), 629–640 (2013)
13. Odelu, V., Das, A.K., Kumari, S., Huang, X., Wazid, M.: Provably secure authenticated key agreement scheme for distributed mobile cloud computing services. Fut. Gen. Comput. Syst. 68, 74–88 (2017)
14. Mohammadali, A., Haghighi, M.S., Tadayon, M.H., Mohammadi-Nodooshan, A.: A novel identity-based key establishment method for advanced metering infrastructure in smart grid. IEEE Trans. Smart Grid 9(4), 2834–2842 (2016)
15. Chen, Y., Martínez, J.F., Castillejo, P., López, L.: An anonymous authentication and key establish scheme for smart grid: FAuth. Energies 10(9), 1354 (2017)
16. Saxena, N., Choi, B.J., Lu, R.: Authentication and authorization scheme for various user roles and devices in smart grid. IEEE Trans. Inf. Foren. Secur. 11(5), 907–921 (2015)
17. Tsai, J.L., Lo, N.W.: Secure anonymous key distribution scheme for smart grid. IEEE Trans. Smart Grid 7(2), 906–914 (2015)
18. He, D., Wang, H., Khan, M.K., Wang, L.: Lightweight anonymous key distribution scheme for smart grid using elliptic curve cryptography. IET Commun. 10(14), 1795–1802 (2016)

19. Gope, P., Sikdar, B.: Privacy-aware authenticated key agreement scheme for secure smart grid communication. IEEE Trans. Smart Grid **10**(4), 3953–3962 (2018)
20. Wazid, M., Das, A.K., Kumar, N., Rodrigues, J.J.: Secure three-factor user authentication scheme for renewable-energy-based smart grid environment. IEEE Trans. Ind. Inform. **13**(6), 3144–3153 (2017)
21. Kumar, P., Gurtov, A., Sain, M., Martin, A., Ha, P.H.: Lightweight authentication and key agreement for smart metering in smart energy networks. IEEE Trans. Smart Grid **10**(4), 4349–4359 (2018)
22. Mahmood, K., Chaudhry, S.A., Naqvi, H., Kumari, S., Li, X., Sangaiah, A.K.: An elliptic curve cryptography based lightweight authentication scheme for smart grid communication. Fut. Gen. Comput. Syst. **81**, 557–565 (2018)
23. Mahmood, K., Li, X., Chaudhry, S.A., Naqvi, H., Kumari, S., Sangaiah, A.K., et al.: Pairing based anonymous and secure key agreement protocol for smart grid edge computing infrastructure. Fut. Gen. Comput. Syst. **88**, 491–500 (2018)
24. Wang, J., Wu, L., Choo, K.K.R., He, D.: Blockchain based anonymous authentication with key management for smart grid edge computing infrastructure. IEEE Trans. Ind. Inform. **16**, 1984–1992 (2019)
25. Garg, S., Kaur, K., Kaddoum, G., Rodrigues, J.J., Guizani, M.: Secure and Lightweight Authentication Scheme for SmartMetering Infrastructure in smart grid. IEEE Trans. Ind. Inform. **16**, 3548–3557 (2019)
26. Jia, X., He, D., Kumar, N., Choo, K.K.R.: A provably secure and efficient identity-based anonymous authentication scheme for mobile edge computing. IEEE Syst. J. **14**, 560–571 (2019)
27. Kahvazadeh, S., Masip-Bruin, X., Diaz, R., Marín-Tordera, E., Jurnet, A., Garcia, J.: Towards an efficient key management and authentication strategy for combined fog-to-cloud continuum systems. In: 2018 3rd Cloudification of the Internet of Things (CIoT), pp. 1–7. IEEE (2018)
28. Zhao, J., Liu, J., Qin, Z., Ren, K.: Privacy protection scheme based on remote anonymous attestation for trusted smart meters. IEEE Trans. Smart Grid **9**(4), 3313–3320 (2016)
29. Zheng, H., Wu, Q., Qin, B., Zhong, L., He, S., Liu, J.: Linkable group signature for auditing anonymous communication. In: Susilo, W., Yang, G. (eds.) ACISP 2018. LNCS, vol. 10946, pp. 304–321. Springer, Cham (2018). https://doi.org/10.1007/978-3-319-93638-3_18
30. Ma, L., Liu, X., Pei, Q., Xiang, Y.: Privacy-preserving reputation management for edge computing enhanced mobile crowdsensing. IEEE Trans. Serv. Comput. **12**(5), 786–799 (2018)
31. Automated Validation of Internet Security Protocols and Applications (AVISPA). http://www.avispa-project.org

Performance Evaluation of Ryu Controller with Weighted Round Robin Load Balancer

Ryhan Uddin[1] and Fahad Monir[2(✉)]

[1] American International University-Bangladesh, Dhaka, Bangladesh
[2] Independent University-Bangladesh, Dhaka, Bangladesh
fahad.monir@iub.edu.bd

Abstract. Current landscape of IT industry is extensively focusing on more control over the intelligent devices within a secured environment while also incorporating cost minimization factor. Therefore Software Defined Networking (SDN) is becoming highly sought after due to its offering of all of these amenities. SDN provides agile networking framework through programmability and reduces the requirements of redundant devices by centralizing single point of control while providing a secured backbone. Various controllers can be used to establish this control over the network. One such controller Ryu shows promising network orchestration features with comprehensive security integrations that allow it to counter most common types of cyber threats directed towards a commercial network. Therefore we have chosen Ryu controller for our project and tried to showcase our work with the implementation of a weighted round robin load balancer with multipath topologies. Afterwards we have tested if the load balancer was precise in calculation of the shortest path and its packet distributions. Then it was estimated how much performance deteriorations occur in terms of raw bandwidth (BW) transmissions between terminals hosts and how much packet loss is incurred when an external middleware (i.e. load balancer) is added in the topology. Our tests showed that the inclusion of the middleware (load balancer in the 3 path topology) caused a peak throughput deterioration of 5.4 Gbits/sec. (from 13.78 Gbits/sec. down to 8.38 Gbits/sec.) and a peak mean value of 1.6010% packet loss therefore, making it evident that higher bandwidth transmissions caused notable performance deteriorations.

Keywords: SDN · Ryu · Load balancer · Mininet · Weighted round robin

1 Introduction

Software Defined Networking (SDN) has enabled robust network orchestration with deep customization through programmability while making it cost effective. Corporate companies are always looking forward to the reduction of costs while maintaining maximum efficiency, which is where SDN comes into play. SDN drastically reduces the number of redundant devices while separating control and data plane in the process. This yields more control for the network admin whilst satisfying the 21st century moto of going Green, because less devices, lesser productions hence lesser emissions.

© Springer Nature Switzerland AG 2021
R. Agrawal et al. (Eds.): ICCEDE 2020, CCIS 1436, pp. 115–129, 2021.
https://doi.org/10.1007/978-3-030-84842-2_9

Current Legacy network suffers from various issue like decentralized control, expensive hardware and firmware, vendor locked features, lack of customization, rigid policy dependency and many more. Network administrator is compelled to micromanage individual devices and policies making the management very hectic with very little to no customization or maneuverability. SDN's advanced framework provides a dynamic view of the network while boasting fine granularity by enabling the use of dynamic rules and customized user defined policies. Moreover, traditional network is vertically integrated hence very hard to expand. With the popularity of Big Data and distributed systems SDN has become more essential than ever. With the segregation of control and data planes SDN enable the Network to be horizontally expanded by adding numerous physical and virtual devices [1]. From Fig. 1 we can see a very basic overview between a traditional Network architecture and SDN architecture.

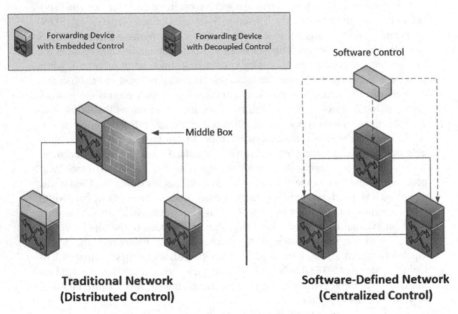

Fig. 1. Traditional network vs SDN network

From Fig. 1 we can observe than traditional Network contains network devices having distributed control and separate middle boxes for multiple segments. As a result Network administrator has to access all the individual devices to configure that specific segment. On the other hand in SDN framework administrator can control all the network nodes (ex: Layer 3 Routers, Switches, Firewalls etc.) from a single controller point where he/she can easily deploy all the configurations, security and networking policies without needing to access singular nodes potentially rendering the nodes as commercial off the shelve devices (COT). This singular controller point is named simply as a controller in SDN. This SDN controller provides full overview of the network and its elements while offering smoother supervision of the network activities and thus putting itself in an objectively favorable position in terms of cybersecurity. SDN controllers enable users to install customized security modules and policies to be used within a network environment with little to no expense in contrast to a traditional network where one firewall can cost big bucks. There are many controllers currently available in the SDN scene hailing from tech giants like CISCO, Brocade, NEC, Juniper etc. each of them competing to come up with the best version of their controllers with all the next generation networking facilities. For our project we have chosen such a versatile controller namely Ryu, because it offers a dynamic and secured platform with seamless integration of security modules, making it a perfect choice for commercial installations. In the later parts of the paper we have discussed briefly on those security aspects. For our work we have tried to evaluate the Ryu controller's performance where a weighted round robin Load balancer was implemented with the script written by Wildan Maulana Syahidillah [2] in combination with our custom topology script in order to incorporate multiple paths and devices within the network. Then it was tested if the packets transmission is properly followed by the weight calculations or not. Afterwards an intensive evolution process was done with the use of iperf [3] tool in order to calculate the deterioration (due to the inclusion of the middleware) in terms of raw bandwidth throughput and packet loss percentage between hosts. Following points summarize the contribution of our project:

- The test results demonstrated that increased numbers of paths and higher bandwidth transmission rates caused notable performance deteriorations.
- A performance assessment was done between our proposed topology and a similarly designed topology [4] using an OpenDaylight (ODL) controller. In comparison, our Ryu controller based setup fared slightly better in terms of raw bandwidth throughput while the load balancer was operational.
- The proposed setup (combination of the Ryu controller, Mininet, load balancer script and our custom topology script) can be used to create a network platform which can offer seamless network expansion where multiple paths and networking devices can be added as per network admin's requirements.

2 Similar Works

Over the past decade various research works have been performed in order to evaluate different SDN controllers. Many of them focused primarily on the raw throughput of the controllers in varying topology conditions adding middleware (i.e. firewalls [5], access points, modular routers [6] and switches, load balancers etc.) while many of them tested out improved techniques, newer compatibilities and policy supports. One such work [7] shows data on evaluations of Ryu controller performance in association with OpenFlow switch while finding various parameters like Bandwidth, Jitter, Packet loss, round trip time etc. In another work [8], authors have used dynamic load balancer within a Ryu controller using Mininet emulation and they have proposed Dijkstra's algorithm in order to find the shortest path and tried to achieve precision in data delivery with minimal latency. There is another research work [9] that focused on establishing static Round robin and random connection based load balancer within a Mininet emulation environment while using the Ryu controller and OpenFlow-enabled switch. Our work is very much akin to this work but we have primarily focused on the weighted round robin load balancer and the overall impact on the throughput of the network with its inclusion. Later we have also tried to measure the precision of the packet distributions and the load balancers path selection accuracy. Another work [4], also focused on a parallel concept where authors have implemented a dynamic load balancing environment with the use of OpenDaylight controller (Nitrogen version) and Mininet for the network orchestration. Afterwards they have used iperf tool to measure the traffic load and the performance of the emulated network just like we did for our throughput measurements. Their first network scenario is very much alike our emulated topology but contains one less device i.e. a Switch. In comparison, our setup (with the Ryu controller and the load balancer) yielded higher throughput rate of 8.82 Gbits/s. even with the extra Hop (one extra Switch) where their topology yielded a throughput rate of 6.6 Gbits/sec with the load balancer. But both setups exhibit reduced yields while more devices and paths are incorporated within the network topology.

3   Background Topics

3.1   SDN Architecture

In Software-Defined Networking the general idea is to provide an open abstraction that divides the Data plane and Control plane while having the network provisioning capabilities of a centralized core controller. The architecture can be categorized into three layers (see Fig. 2). The Application layer mainly utilized various business APIs (application program interface) which are openly developed by various application developers. It allows open apps while leveraging network information like network state, topology structures, uplink statistics etc. therefore allowing seamless development for various scenarios like network automation, mass policy implementation, link troubleshooting, security implementation and network supervision. To name a few of these apps: Brocade Network Advisor and Flow Optimizer, HPE Network Visualizer, Aricent SDN Load balancer, TechM smart flow steering etc. [10]. These Apps are mainly utilized with REST APIs through the northbound interface which connects the controller with the application layer. Control layer is the Plane where the brain of network aka controller resides. This controller takes all the logical decisions while boasting unhindered network orchestration capabilities. It uses southbound interface and utilizes southbound APIs like OpenFlow, Ovsdb, Netconf to connect with the infrastructure layer. The infrastructure layer contains all the forwarding devices, the COTs (commercial off the shelf devices), the White boxes, switches, routers etc. where the underlying physical network resides. The controller can lay down the virtual framework upon this physical network potentially modifying it on the process.

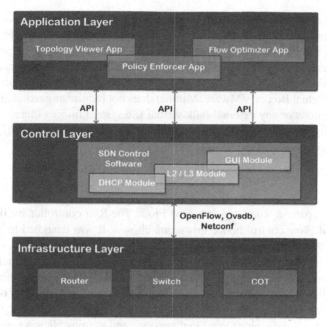

Fig. 2. Traditional network vs SDN network

3.2 Controller

In an SDN framework the controller acts as the primary core that facilitates supervision over the different network elements and all in all satisfies the notion of a programmable abstraction by splitting forwarding plane from control plane. This supervision is achieved through controller that exemplifies unconstrained autonomy in Network design. The controller also performs operations like: API interfacing, session control, network and flow management and network modeling etc. which aids in unhindered network control. There are many controllers in the market each satisfying their own networking ventures with custom environments and varying amenities. Some popular open controllers are POX/NOX, OpenDaylight (ODL), Beacon, Ryu, Floodlight, ONOS, Faucet, OpenContrail etc. There are also controllers which are developed and marketed commercially. To name a few The Brocade SDN controller, NEC, VMware (vCloud), Nicira, Contrail/Juniper etc. are the most popular ones [11].

3.3 Mininet

Mininet [12] is a Linux based emulator that provides dynamic platform to emulate different virtual scenarios associating various network elements like routers, switches, SDN controllers, firewalls etc. [13]. It is designed to attain functional fidelity and scalability while executing raw network codes within lightweight Linux Containers. Due to its support of OpenFlow based SDN elements like: OpenVSwtich, OpenFlow protocol etc. It is widely adopted within the SDN community for network simulations. It enables easy custom topology orchestrations using Python scripts with decent accuracy and hence is a perfect and inexpensive tool for prototyping and debugging [12]. Mininet offers testbed that can run simultaneous projects on multiple terminals while supporting up to 4096 hosts on single machine. Precision is one of Mininet's creation principals where design and management of a virtual network resembles to its physical counterpart hence providing accurate outputs similar to a real physical network. It can be run on Any OS that supports Virtual Box or VMware. Mininet does not require any redundant software, kernels or daemons or any external bulk virtual file system images therefore making it substantially lightweight, fast and can be seamlessly integrated into multiple physical servers for resource clustering.

3.4 Ryu

Ryu [14] is a Japanese word which means Flow. The Ryu controller itself was aimed to make use of Flow control hence this name chosen. It was designed to be agile and lightweight while also supporting adaptive network virtualization. Ryu is supported by Nippon Telegraph and Telephone Corp. (NTT) and is also being used as their Data Center backbone based on Ryu controller based SDN framework. It is a python based open source controller and its code is attainable with the Apache license. Ryu offers a huge support of protocols like various southbound protocols like: OpenFlow, Ovsdb, Netconf. It supports all the major OpenFlow versions and various Niciria extensions. Ryu controller supports various network devices namely NEC PF5220, HP 2920, IBM Rack-Switch G8264, Trema Switch, Indigo Virtual Switch which are all OpenFlow based and frequently used in commercial networking operations. For our work we have exclusively chosen Ryu controller because its monolithic architecture is very proficient in countering most common types of cyberattacks like Brute force attack and Denial of service (DOS). According to a quarterly report [15] published in Sept. 2017 by McAfee Labs states that these two attacks are one of the most common types of threats that are encountered worldwide where Brute force attack holds 20% of the total threat types and DOS holds around 15%. The Ryu controller allows the integration of Snort module [16] (developed by Sourcefire) which offers Intrusion detection system and Intrusion prevention system that tackle the Brute force attacks with ease. Moreover, according to the work of [17] the later versions of Ryu controller (Version 4.0) have minimal DOS attack index which are the lowest among many other popular SDN controllers like OpenDaylight, Floodlight, POX etc.

4 Primary Experiment

In our experiment the main goal was to create a virtual network using Mininet emulator where 2 hosts were taken with multiple OpenFlow switches in order to create distinct routing paths. Ryu was used as the remote controller in order to run the whole network. We used the load balancer script which was written by Wildan Maulana Syahidillah [2] and created additional path for testing out the scripts efficiency. Then we have calculated bandwidth transmission rates and Packet loss between the two hosts for two and three routing paths sequentially. Finally we have compared all the values for variable time frames and multiple bandwidth (BW) conditions.

4.1 Network Setup

For our experiment Virtual Box was used as the virtual platform. The hardware is powered with an Intel core i7 6700 CPU having the clock speed of 3.40 GHz, 8 GB RAM with a base operating system of Ubuntu ver. 18.04 LTS 64 bit. For the network emulation we used Mininet version 2.2, Miniedit (within Mininet) for topology formation and Ryu as the remote controller. 2 hosts were created namely host 1 (h1) and hosts 2 (h2) where h1 had an IP address of 10.0.0.1 and h2 had an IP address of 10.0.0.2. A total of 8 OpenFlow switches namely s1, s2, s3, s4, s5, s6, s7, s8 were used in the network. All of these switches were used to create distinct paths with multiple hops in order test out whether the load balancer could efficiently calculate its path or not. The paths were segregated with 2 terminal switches directly connecting with two hosts. First path had only one switch named s2 connecting to the terminal switches, the second path had 2 switches connecting to the terminal switches and the third and final path had a total of three switches. Then we have calculated BW transmission rate and packet loss between two hosts (with and without the load balancer scripts). Following two figures (see Fig. 3 and Fig. 4) shows the network topologies that were used for the test runs.

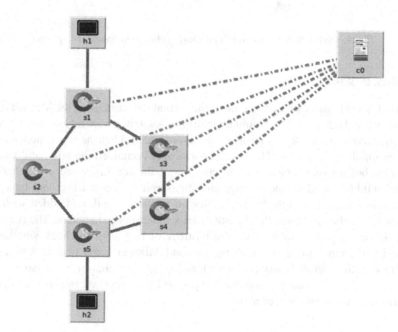

Fig. 3. Network Setup of weighted round robin load balancer (2 paths)

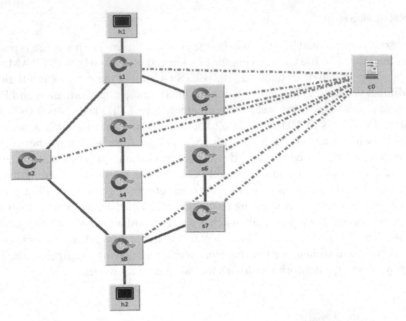

Fig. 4. Network Setup of weighted round robin load balancer (3 paths)

4.2 Work Process

The experiments began with the creation of the virtual Network using the Mininet having two hosts h1 and h2. Then two terminal OpenFlow switches were added with these two hosts respectively and the Ryu controller was incorporated. Then the experiment was split into three topology scenarios. The first scenario only contained the hosts and switches (two Paths) but we kept it basic without any load balancer. In the second scenario we included Wildan's load balancer script and measured the packet loss and bandwidth transmission rates between the hosts. Finally an additional path was added with three switches which then followed the measurements of similar parameters. The reason for adding this extra path is to increase the number of hops and to check whether this increased hop count can be weighted by the load balancer script or not. Additionally how it impacts the overall throughput of the topology. Afterwards we have also measured similar parameters (i.e. transmission rate and packet loss percentage) and made a detailed comparison between all the scenarios.

4.3 Work Flow

The work flow starts with the launch of Mininet fetching the topology structure from Miniedit. The controller Ryu was defined as a Core remote controller for topology supervision and Open vSwitch Kernel mode was set by default. For this experiment OpenFlow version 1.3 was used. After the topology went live the "pingall" command was used to populate the flow table. Both the hosts sent ICMP packets though the topology routes where negotiations were made with each of the OpenFlow Switches. Hence there was an initial delay right after the table miss event. After the initial propagation was done the flows were cached by the controller therefore making further propagations faster. Then we have instantiated the Ryu load balancer python script by Wildan on a separate CLI terminal. The script instantiates the multipath load balancing mechanism where the controller now calculates bucket weights for individual routing paths. Each of these paths are assigned with calculated bucket weight numbers. Ideally the shortest path is the best path to put forward more of the packets to yield best performance. So first the shortest path is calculated by the controller counting the hops. We can observe the shortest path calculations (for 3 paths) from the following Fig. 5.

```
switch_features_handler is called
Available paths from  1  to  8  :   [[1, 5, 6, 7, 8], [1, 3, 4, 8], [1, 2, 8]]
[1, 2, 8] cost =  2
[1, 3, 4, 8] cost =  3
Path installation finished in  0.0159118175507
Available paths from  8  to  1  :   [[8, 7, 6, 5, 1], [8, 4, 3, 1], [8, 2, 1]]
[8, 2, 1] cost =  2
[8, 4, 3, 1] cost =  3
Path installation finished in  0.00707793235779
Available paths from  8  to  1  :   [[8, 7, 6, 5, 1], [8, 4, 3, 1], [8, 2, 1]]
[8, 2, 1] cost =  2
[8, 4, 3, 1] cost =  3
Path installation finished in  0.0192210674286
```

Fig. 5. Shortest path calculation (3 paths)

From the Fig. 5 we can see that first path [1, 2, 8] has the lowest hop cost (i.e. 2) hence it is the shortest path. Therefore this shortest path is assigned with a higher bucket weight value. Then the packets are distributed while favoring the higher bucket valued path and also sending lesser amount of packets through the longer path (lesser bucket weight) as well. By using "ovs-ofctl -O OpenFlow dump-groups" command we can view the assigned bucket weight value for the shortest paths within the topology. The following figure shows us the outputs. From the Fig. 6 and Fig. 7 we can see that shortest path (remarked by s8-eth2) is the shortest way out from s8 (from switch 8 perspective). Hence it gets the highest weight value of 6.

```
bickey@bickey-VirtualBox:~$ sudo ovs-ofctl -O OpenFlow13 dump-groups
OFPST_GROUP_DESC reply (OF1.3) (xid=0x2):
 group_id=4131401741,type=select,bucket=weight:6,watch_port:"s8-eth2"
```

Fig. 6. Bucket weight for shortest path

Next the Xterm was used to access both the hosts h1 and h2 where we have declared the h1 as the server that accepts packets from associated ports and h2 as the client that send packets (through Switch 8 i.e. s8). Then for the bandwidth measurement tool iperf was used for various BW conditions while simultaneously using multiple ports to send bulk amount of packets. Followings are two different screenshots of two packet transmission scenarios where the load balancer chooses to transmit more packets through its preferred shortest path i.e. s8-eth2. See the Fig. 8 and Fig. 9.

```
actions=output:"s8-eth2",bucket=weight:4,watch_port:"s8-eth3",actions
```

Fig. 7. Longer path yields lesser bucket weight

```
bickey@bickey-VirtualBox:~$ sudo ovs-ofctl -O OpenFlow13 dump-ports s8
OFPST_PORT reply (OF1.3) (xid=0x2): 5 ports
  port LOCAL: rx pkts=0, bytes=0, drop=1, errs=0, frame=0, over=0, crc=0
              tx pkts=0, bytes=0, drop=0, errs=0, coll=0
              duration=1107.058s
  port "s8-eth4": rx pkts=976, bytes=60299, drop=0, errs=0, frame=0, over=0, crc=0
              tx pkts=975, bytes=60257, drop=0, errs=0, coll=0
              duration=1107.075s
  port "s8-eth1": rx pkts=568427, bytes=28789340546, drop=0, errs=0, frame=0, over=0, crc=0
              tx pkts=249591, bytes=16470489, drop=0, errs=0, coll=0
              duration=1107.077s
  port "s8-eth2": rx pkts=197222, bytes=13012315, drop=0, errs=0, frame=0, over=0, crc=0
              tx pkts=402962, bytes=19979550719, drop=0, errs=0, coll=0
              duration=1107.072s
  port "s8-eth3": rx pkts=53343, bytes=3518333, drop=0, errs=0, frame=0, over=0, crc=0
              tx pkts=167391, bytes=8809908969, drop=0, errs=0, coll=0
              duration=1107.080s
```

Fig. 8. Scenario 1: higher packet transfer rate (Tx) through preferred path (i.e. s8-eth2)

```
bickey@bickey-VirtualBox:~$ sudo ovs-ofctl -O OpenFlow13 dump-ports s8
[sudo] password for bickey:
OFPST_PORT reply (OF1.3) (xid=0x2): 5 ports
  port LOCAL: rx pkts=0, bytes=0, drop=1, errs=0, frame=0, over=0, crc=0
              tx pkts=0, bytes=0, drop=0, errs=0, coll=0
              duration=7691.466s
  port "s8-eth4": rx pkts=7479, bytes=450603, drop=0, errs=0, frame=0, over=0, crc=0
              tx pkts=7479, bytes=450621, drop=0, errs=0, coll=0
              duration=7691.482s
  port "s8-eth1": rx pkts=1545726, bytes=78173514068, drop=0, errs=0, frame=0, over=0, crc=0
              tx pkts=756139, bytes=49867003, drop=0, errs=0, coll=0
              duration=7691.484s
  port "s8-eth2": rx pkts=542370, bytes=35755813, drop=0, errs=0, frame=0, over=0, crc=0
              tx pkts=1102232, bytes=55262273015, drop=0, errs=0, coll=0
              duration=7691.479s
  port "s8-eth3": rx pkts=221247, bytes=14561723, drop=0, errs=0, frame=0, over=0, crc=0
              tx pkts=458424, bytes=22912140643, drop=0, errs=0, coll=0
              duration=7691.487s
```

Fig. 9. Scenario 2: higher packet transfer rate (Tx) through preferred path (i.e. s8-eth2)

As we can observe from the above figures that both scenarios show the preferred path s8-eth2 is transmitting more packets than the other paths. So the screenshots testify that the implemented load balancer for three separate routing paths is working just as intended. But working with the script we have found out that when we tried to ping an unknown host in the topology (for example: 10.0.0.100) the controller flooded the topology with ARP loops. So it requires some improvements in regards to ARP handling.

Finally we have logged the output results for a detailed performance evaluation for both load balancing and Non load balancing scenarios. The following flow chart (see Fig. 10) shows the whole process in simple steps.

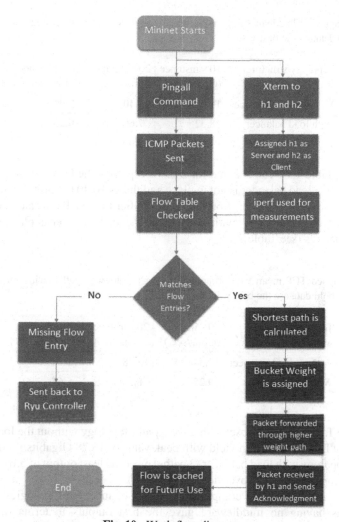

Fig. 10. Work flow diagram

4.4 Results and Evaluations

For evaluation we have focused on two parameters in two separate phases: bandwidth (BW) and packet loss. In first phase for BW measurement we have used the iperf and evaluated transmission rates for the topology in both scenarios (with and without load balancer) while putting no restriction on maximum bandwidth (uncapped). We have used Transmission Control Protocol (TCP) and calculated values of three different instances for 10 s, 20 s and 30 s respectively for both 2 paths and 3 paths topology structures. The resultant value of each instance is a mean value of five separate runs which ensured more precision in the outputs. Following Table 1 provides the data transfer rate for Topology with and without load balancer for 2 paths.

Table 1. Uncapped TCP Mean value (BW) for Topology (2 paths) with and without the load balancer (bold data are the best value)

Topology structure with Ryu controller	10 s instance (Gbits/sec.)	20 s instance (Gbits/sec.)	30 s instance (Gbits/Sec.)
Without load balancer	11.08	**16.40**	12.90
With load balancer	8.32	7.66	**10.23**

From the Table 1 we can see that for 2 paths topology the best transmission rate is attained when the load balancer is not in place and that is 16.40 Gigabits/s and with load balancer the output is as low as 7.66 Gigabits/s. After this we have calculated similar parameters for 3 paths topology with and without the load balancer in place for the two topology structures (see Table 2).

Table 2. Uncapped TCP mean value (bandwidth) for topology (3 paths) with and without the load balancer (bold data are the best value)

Topology structure with Ryu controller	10 s instance (Gbits/sec.)	20 s instance (Gbits/sec.)	30 s instance (Gbits/sec.)
Without load balancer	10.34	**13.78**	12.40
With load balancer	**9.25**	8.38	5.67

From the Table 2 we can observe that for 3 paths topology without the load balancer it has the best BW transmission yield with peak value of 13.78 Gigabits/second. On the other hand topology with load balancer (3 paths) gives the least output of 5.67 Gigabits/s. Following Graph gives better overview (see Fig. 11).

So overall from the above comparisons we can deduce that topologies with lesser routing paths having no middleware gave the best outputs in terms of uncapped transmission rates.

For our next phase, we have measured the packet loss for each of the network setups (i.e. With and without load balancer) while using User Datagram Protocol (UDP) to send packets from one host to another under specific BW limits of 500 Mbps, 600 Mbps, 700 Mbps, 800 Mbps and 1000 Mbps respectively. Just like the previous calculations we have taken mean value for multiple runs and then compared the data for more accuracy. The Next table gives the detailed Comparison between topologies having 2 paths for both load balancing and no load balancing scenarios (see Table 3).

From the Table 3 we can see that the best performance was achieved when the topology had no middleware and it had the least amount of packet loss which is 0.0041% and on the other hand with load balancer the loss is the highest and that is 1.2008% which might add up significantly when there will be simultaneous connections (due to mass user activity) in data center networks. In our next table we have shown the comparison for 3 paths topology with and without the load balancer (see Table 4).

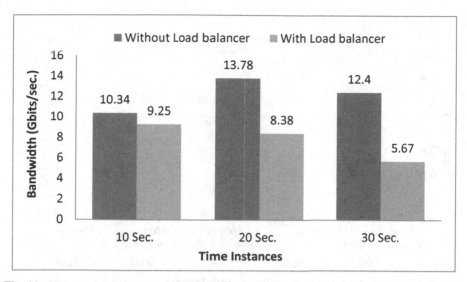

Fig. 11. Uncapped TCP mean value for topology with 3 paths (with and without load balancer)

Table 3. UDP mean value (packet loss) for topology (2 paths) with and without the load balancer (bold data are the best value)

Topology structure with Ryu controller	500 Mbps	600 Mbps	700 Mbps	800 Mbps	1000 Mbps
Without load balancer	0.0068%	0.0079%	**0.0041%**	0.0156%	0.0198%
With load balancer	0.0159%	**0.0085%**	1.2008%	0.7700%	0.0531%

Table 4. UDP mean value (packet loss) for topology (3 paths) with and without the load balancer (bold data are the best value)

Topology structure with Ryu controller	500 Mbps	600 Mbps	700 Mbps	800 Mbps	1000 Mbps
Without load balancer	0.0082%	**0.0066%**	0.0094%	0.0191%	0.0322%
With load balancer	**0.0411%**	0.0998%	1.1053%	0.8620%	1.6010%

From above Table 4 we can observe that incorporating the middleware (i.e. load balancer) caused packet loss in terms of higher BW parameters. With the load balancer in place the topology yielded the highest mean value of 1.6010% packet loss when 3 routing paths were introduced. But without the middleware packet loss is very minimal, 0.0322% being the worst case scenario. The Following Graph gives a clearer picture of our observations (see Fig. 12).

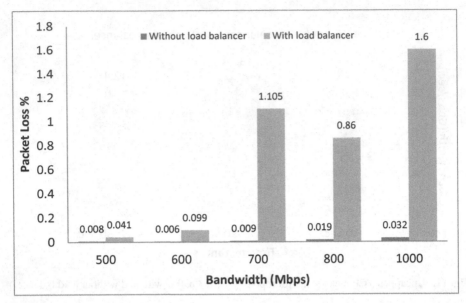

Fig. 12. UDP Mean value (packet loss) for topology with 3 paths (with and without load balancer)

So from the above observations we can summarize that the inclusion of the middleware (i.e. load balancer) did cause overall performance deteriorations in terms of uncapped bandwidth transmission rate and also incurred more packet loss. We have also observed that additional routing paths also impacted on the overall performance of the topologies. Although in the current network setup these factors might seem very trivial but they can prove substantial in terms of large data center networks where thousands of users are communicating simultaneously.

5 Conclusion

With the advancements of current era it is high time that we reduced our carbon footprints by following a minimalistic hardware production system. From that perspective SDN can play a vital role by enabling more options with less hardware while also providing secured and open platform with the supervision of a powerful controller. One such controller Ryu shows much promise and gained a lot of popularity in SDN scene. Through our work we have found out that for multi path topology Ryu trades exceptionally well even with externally incorporated middleware (i.e. load balancer in our case). But it does show very minimal performance deterioration with the inclusion of such an external entity. Moreover, we have found that introducing additional routing paths also impacts adversely on the overall throughput of the topology and incurs significant packet loss. Therefore network admins should be cautious while working in larger data centric networks as these factors might hinder in terms of high volume user activity. For our future work, we can focus on refining the load balancer where it can be more effective for large data centers that might be consisting of 10 to 20 paths having equally numbered Hops and also it can be compatible with multiple platforms.

References

1. Xia, W., Wen, Y., Foh, C., Niyato, D., Xie, H.: A survey on software-defined networking. IEEE Commun. Surveys Tutorials **17**, 27–51 (2015)
2. Syahidillah, W.: wildan2711 - Overview, https://github.com/wildan2711
3. GUEANT, V.: iPerf - The TCP, UDP and SCTP network bandwidth measurement tool, https://iperf.fr
4. Nkosi, M., Lysko, A., Dlamini, S.: Multi-path load balancing for SDN data plane. In: 2018 International Conference on Intelligent and Innovative Computing Applications (ICONIC) (2018)
5. Uddin, R., Monir, M.: Evaluation of four SDN controllers with firewall modules. In: Proceedings of the International Conference on Computing Advancements (2020)
6. Monir, M., Uddin, R., Pan, D.: Behavior of NAPT middleware in an SDN environment. In: 2019 4th International Conference on Electrical Information and Communication Technology (EICT) (2019)
7. Islam, M.T., Islam, N., Refat, M.A.: Node to node performance evaluation through RYU SDN controller. Wireless Pers. Commun. **112**(1), 555–570 (2020). https://doi.org/10.1007/s11277-020-07060-4
8. Tiwari, G., Chakaravarthy, V., Rai, A.: dynamic load balancing in software defined networking. Int. J. Eng. Adv. Technol. **8**, 2706–2712 (2019)
9. Hamed, M., ElHalawany, B., Fouda, M., Eldien, A.: Performance analysis of applying load balancing strategies on different SDN environments. Benha J. Appl. Sci. **2**, 91–97 (2017)
10. Arora, H.: Software Defined Networking (SDN) - Architecture and role of Open-Flow, https://www.howtoforge.com/tutorial/software-defined-networking-sdn-architecture-and-role-of-openflow
11. What are SDN Controllers (or SDN Controller Platforms)?, https://www.sdxcentral.com/networking/sdn/definitions/sdn-controllers
12. Team, M.: Mininet: An Instant Virtual Network on your Laptop (or other PC) - Mininet, http://mininet.org
13. Keti, F., Askar, S.: Emulation of software defined networks using Mininet in different simulation environments. In: 2015 6th International Conference on Intelligent Systems, Modelling and Simulation (2015)
14. https://osrg.github.io/ryu-book/en/Ryubook.pdf
15. Top 8 Network Attacks by Type in 2017, https://www.calyptix.com/top-threats/top-8-network-attacks-type-2017
16. Snort Intergration Ryu 4.34 Documentation, https://ryu.readthedocs.io/en/latest/snort_integrate.html
17. Wu, Z., Wei, Q.: Quantitative analysis of the security of software-defined network controller using threat/effort model. Math. Probl. Eng. **2017**, 1–11 (2017)

An IoT Based Intelligent Control System for Physically Disabled People

C. Ramesh[✉] ⓘ, E. Udayakumarⓘ, K. Yogeshwaranⓘ, and P. Omprakashⓘ

Department of ECE, KIT-Kalaignarkarunanidhi Institute of Technology, Coimbatore, Tamilnadu, India

Abstract. Smart wheelchairs have been created for quite a while to help incapacitated individuals with a few inability levels. Much of the time, the eye muscles of incapacitated individuals are one of only a handful couple of controllable muscles that still capacity well. In this way, utilizing the eye-stare as an interface for deadened or physically crippled individuals has been of intrigue. The proposed framework exhibits the IoT based control System for physically Disabled People. It means to give a doable answer for physically impaired individuals who don't be able to move the wheelchair and to control the different home apparatuses without anyone else. These incorporate individuals with genuine incapacitated condition. In this eye following based innovation, three Proximity Infrared sensor are mounted on an eye casing to follow the development of the iris. Since, IR sensors distinguish just white items, an interesting arrangement of computerized bits is produced relating to each eye development. These IoT based sign are then prepared by means of arduino controller IC to control the engines of the wheelchair. To control the Home apparatuses transfers are utilized with the Arduino. The potential and effectiveness of recently created restoration frameworks that utilization head motion control, jaw control, taste n-puff control, voice acknowledgment, and EEG flag variedly have likewise been investigated in detail. They were observed to be awkward as they served either constrained ease of use or non-moderateness. After different relapse examinations, the proposed plan was created as a savvy, adaptable and stream-lined option for individuals who experience difficulty embracing ordinary assistive advancements. The proposed IoT based control systems is used to control the overall operation of physically disabled persons.

Keywords: Arduino · IoT · Watchdog timer · Proximity sensor · Infrared sensor

1 Introduction

Wheelchairs were structured with the plan to push physically crippled individuals to move around and achieve day by day life undertakings. An ever-increasing number of advances in innovations fresher and more intelligent wheelchairs are coming into the market to support the seriously crippled people. Physically tested people find trouble in power ON/OFF their home loads, for example, fan, light, AC and so on, they require an attender to do these things. Without the attender their reality is by all accounts progressively troublesome. So, a plan which can assist them with powering ON/OFF their home burdens indeed, even without an attender will be very fundamental. With visual

© Springer Nature Switzerland AG 2021
R. Agrawal et al. (Eds.): ICCEDE 2020, CCIS 1436, pp. 130–140, 2021.
https://doi.org/10.1007/978-3-030-84842-2_10

perception being their direct, the incapacitated would spare vitality and could utilize their hands and arms for other exercises [1].

There are no items existing, yet there are dissimilar applications, for example, computer created reality utilizing eye next to control the vision of the game [3]. Eye following is not intensely utilized in standard items but rather are starting to get as contribution to gadgets become increasingly regular. The motivation behind this undertaking is to create a wheelchair that will be constrained by the eye development of the individual situated in the [22] wheelchair and furthermore to control the home apparatuses through eye development. These incorporate individuals with genuine disabled condition. It is constrained by retina development. The eye development is estimated by eyeball sensor. A IoT ultrasonic sensor is utilized to identify the obstructions before the seat. The sign from the sensors are prepared, and the wheel seat is controlled by Arduino controller. The IoT based IR transmitter is utilized to move the developments of eyeball sensor to the IR collector, at that point the home machines are constrained by utilizing the transfer circuit [4].

The utilization of infrared innovation assumes a basic job in eye following as it permits. one to draw associations from a mental viewpoint between eye development information and neurological procedures in the cerebrum. In this proposed plan, an eye mounted casing has been built up that is worn like displays [21]. The last piece of the undertaking is the engine drivers to interface with the wheelchair itself. There IoT based two engine drivers for each engine on the wheelchair both left and right wheels. Each engine driver will comprise of a h-connect that self-control the engine relying upon the yield of the controller. The engine drivers will control both speed and course to empower the wheelchair to push ahead, invert, left and right [6].

The previously mentioned encourages the individual to move freely in the equivalent way this venture likewise proposes to get to the home appliances, for example, fan, light and so forth by the development of the retina. This is made conceivable by utilizing eye ball sensors and transfer. Transfer here goes about as change to work the gadgets. What's more we have moreover included a sound playback framework with the goal that the sound is delivered if there should be an occurrence of crisis. This is finished with the worry about seriously loss of motion patients in light of the fact that their wellbeing condition may fluctuate time to time and they may feel entirely awkward on the off chance that they are constantly in work. In the event that such cases happen the crisis voice [2] which is pre-recorded is played with the goal that it is demonstrated to the people in charge.

2 Related Works

This strategic an effectively relevant and practically feasible framework for home robotization that can be actualized with constrained changes to the current home arrangement. At the equivalent time the framework will likewise be basic satisfactory from clients discernment and subsequently can likewise be utilized by any normal people. The task points mean of home computerization utilizing Zigbee module which can be worked from home. The home machine on getting signal from the Zigbee module works as per the got order. The utilization of Zigbee has a great deal of favorable circumstances. Zigbee is a remote convention similar and generally advanced than Bluetooth [20].

Further the Zigbee worked with various frameworks can convey at the equivalent time with no effect and consequently increments more prominent operationality. The undertaking can be used to deal with any outer condition where in the individual may jump at the chance to control his whole environment, for example, fans, lights, TVs, and so forth; He may likewise prefer to discharge the entryway [23] for somebody or lock the water tap. Every single one these should be possible by utilizing basic guidelines and the individual needs to simply give expert in the PC. A computerized framework is to be created to control the engine turn of wheel seat dependent on head and finger development of truly tested individual. In request to encourage these individuals for their autonomous development, an accelerometer gadget is fitted on people head and a flex sensor is fixed in a glove which is to be wear by the individual. In light of the head and finger developments the accelerometer and the flex sensor will drive the engine fitted to the wheel seat. The wheel seat can be driven in any of the four bearings [27].

A significant part in the IoT is the assortment of sensors that distinguish physical, compound, and natural changes as occasions and report them mathematically. Using a wide range of kinds of sensors assists with improving the nature of data. IoT has a amazing capacity in thinking and perceiving this present reality circumstance, yet the momentous thing is the correspondence work. Contrasted and the past pervasive framework, information transmission is truly steady [29]. IoT has advanced in itself and has been utilized in different fields to cause reformist change. There is a checked distinction among past and keen medical services. The previous starts analysis and treatment simply after a patient with a manifestation visit a specialist, while the last starts them, despite the fact that an indication doesn't yet show up or a patient doesn't visit a specialist. This has not been conceded up until now, as per good judgment of clinical framework. In like manner, shrewd vehicles showed up, when IoT, Big Data and AI are merged with vehicles. They are not just forward leap, in that they are thoughtfully unique in relation to the current ones, yet additionally creative [32] items which instigate changes even in street and metropolitan condition. In this manner, IoT, Big Data and AI have brought about extremely new and thrilling changes over every mechanical area.

The use IoT for crisis correspondence when an crisis circumstance happens. The utilization of what can be utilized to perceive different complex circumstances in reality as a basic specialized instrument is vital for harshly debilitated individuals who are hard to convey and impart. There are different sorts of handicaps. Some are truly sound, others are hard to convey, and some have scholarly movement that doesn't meddle; however, the physical capacity is fundamentally debilitated. A few issues are portrayed by exceptionally incomplete incapacity of the body's capacity, yet extreme weakness or serious useful debilitation is likewise present. As of late, there have been fires in the homes [28] of handicapped individuals in Korea, yet there have been situations where an individual couldn't clear because of a physical incapacity that could have been cleared adequately. The handicapped individual who had a mishap couldn't clear despite the fact that he had the option to act gradually, and needed more an ideal opportunity to utilize the correspondence gear. There are much more extreme cases among individuals with physical handicaps, and for this situation, correspondence should be made sure about in a crisis [31].

Applications

IoT is arrangement of related sensors, registering and advanced gadgets spread over the globe over the web which can convey among them to share and move data utilizing novel id which is allocated to each and each gadget, as UIDs (Unique Identifiers). With the developing of various business premises and social orders, the concentration to mechanize these premises have expanded radically [30]. Likewise, the developing traffic jumble in the urban areas has pushed everybody towards a superior and more dependable electrical control framework. An easy to understand web application and versatile based reconnaissance and control framework associated with IOT cloud worker is utilized here formore vitality conservation and early goal if there should arise an occurrence of any shortcoming recognition. In this new developing time where brilliant urban areas are taking into shape, the exertion for ideal vitality-based traffic light and light control framework has picked up pace. So, exertion has been taken to give a dependable furthermore, easy to use application for simple to utilize and screen the electrical gadgets. The proposed IoT system is dedicated for elderly, disable peoples, handicapped persons and others [25].

3 System Design

The proposed IoT framework intends to give a plausible answer for physically. In capacitated individuals who don't be able to move the wheelchair and to control the different home machines without anyone else. These incorporate individuals [23] with genuine disabled condition.

A) IR Sensor

The IR sensors are utilized to quantify the eye development to control the wheel seat and home appliances. It is utilized to quantify the warmth of the item. The IoT based Infrared (IR) innovation tends to an expansive collection of wireless requests, mainly in the zones of sensing and remote control. The present most up to date items such as cell telephones, computerized cameras, and DVD players as well as remote controls for each market fragment depend on IR sensing and control gadgets. IR sensors distinguish just white items, an interesting arrangement of computerized 8 bits are introduced. ROHM Semiconductor has been driving innovation propels that have prompted a growing number of IR detecting and communication applications for more than 40 years [10] (Fig. 1).

B) DC Motor

The most generally perceived sorts rely upon the forces conveyed by alluring fields. Right around a wide scope of DC motors [22] have a couple of internal instrument, either electromechanical or electronic, to discontinuously change the heading of current stream in part of the motor. Most sorts produce spinning development; a straight motor really makes force and development in an orderly fashion. DC motors were the chief kind by and large used, since they could be controlled from existing direct-current lighting power course systems [6].

C) ROHM Semiconductor IR Solutions

ROHM Semiconductor offers a few items to address each kind of IR gadget innovation. A couple of key items show an expansive scope of capabilities with an exceptional

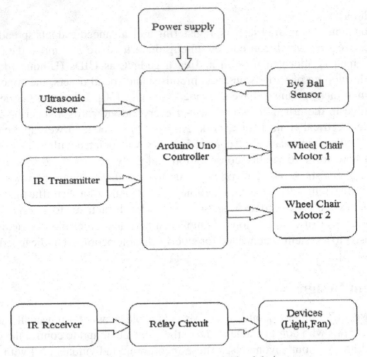

Fig. 1. Block diagram of proposed wheelchair system

spotlight on packaging. IR Emitters ROHM Semiconductor IR optical sensor innovation covers infrared light discharging diodes (LEDs). A few items are accessible in both surface mount (SMD) and through-opening (THD) designs. Leap forward IR wavelength producer [7] innovation has come about in the improvement of IR producers that work close 850 nm. Phototransistors have a wide transmission capacity yet with a pinnacle affectability at around 800 nm. The 850 nm level is a lot nearer to this pinnacle affectability (contrasted and regular producers that work near 950 nm), bringing about higher yield proficiency and a vitality investment funds of 66%. The new SIM-040ST shows an improved pinnacle wavelength (870 nm) and high IR power yield in a 1.6 × 2.25 × 3.1 mm SMD bundle. The SIM-030ST with comparative execution is offered in a much more slender (0.9 mm) and littler.

D) IR Phototransistors/Sensors
ROHM Semiconductor IR phototransistors include high increase and high gatherer current in an assortment of bundling alternatives. For instance, the SCM-014TB is a top-see formed sort with focal point intended for programmed mounting and SMD reflow get together, while the SML-810TB is a shaped sort focal point plan good with turn around mounting. The RPM-012PB is a high affectability, side view sensor offered in a ultra-little 2 × 3 × 2 mm surface mount bundle including a surrounding light channel, making it a perfect match with the SIM-012SB photograph producer [4].

E) Transformer

If the assistant has less turns in the twist, by then the fundamental, the discretionary twist's voltage will lessen and the current or AMPS will increase or decreased depend on the wire check. This is known as a STEP-DOWN transformer. By then the assistant of the potential transformer will be related with the rectifier.

F) Ultrasonic Sensor

It is utilized to detect the snag before the seat, figures the separation by delivering ultrasonic waves [1]. It has a ultrasonic transmitter and a collector. Ultrasonic sensors are most usually utilized in the diffuse mode. A solitary ultrasonic transducer is utilized as both producer and collector and is ordinarily contained in same lodging as the assessment gadgets [8].

G) Relay

To control the Home apparatuses transfers are utilized with the Arduino. Transfers moreover used to run the engine through the controller. It goes about as a switch. The transfer remains in regularly shut state. At the point when transfer loops are empowered the hand-off changes from regularly shut to ordinarily open state because of electromagnetic enlistment [24].

4 Results and Discussion

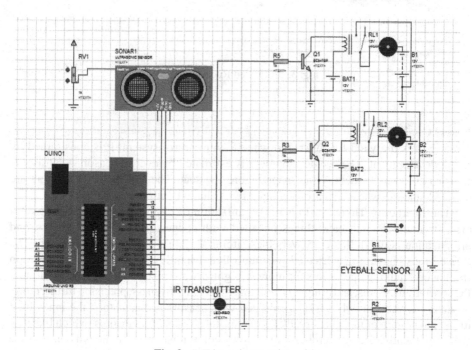

Fig. 2. IoT based transmitter side

Transmitter

The above Fig. 2 shows the simulation result of IoT based transmitter side. In this the eyeball sensor is associated with the arduino controller to give the info, in light of the eye development the engine will keep running by utilizing DC engine and hand-off circuit.

Receiver

The IoT based receiver side is shown in Fig. 3, in this figure IR recipient is utilized to get the sign from IR transmitter to control the home apparatuses rough the hand-off circuit.

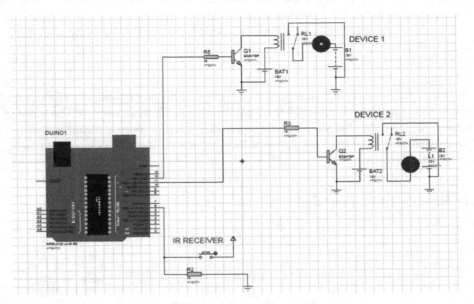

Fig. 3. IoT based Receiver side

Wheel Chair Control

The Fig. 4 is the yield for IoT based wheel chair control system. It is constrained by retina development. The eye development is estimated by eyeball sensor. A ultrasonic sensor is utilized to identify the snags before the seat. The sign from the sensors are handled, and the wheel seat is constrained by Arduino controller.

The Internet of Things (IoT) is the organization of physical articles gadgets, vehicles, structures and different things installed with gadgets programming sensors, and organization network that empowers these items to gather and trade information. The IOT permits objects to be detected and controlled distantly across existing organization framework, making open doors for more straightforward mix of the physical world into PC based frameworks, and bringing about improved effectiveness, precision furthermore, monetary advantage; when IOT is enlarged with sensors and actuators, the innovation turns into an case of the more broad class of digital physical frameworks, which likewise incorporates advancements, for example, savvy condition networks, shrewd homes, wise transportation and savvy urban areas. Everything is exceptionally recognizable through its implanted registering framework yet can interoperate inside the current Internet framework. Specialists gauge that the IoT will comprise of very nearly 50 billion items by 2020 IoT gadgets can be utilized to screen and control the mechanical, electrical and electronic frameworks utilized in different kinds of structures in home robotization.

Fig. 4. For IoT based wheel chair control system

When IoT is applied, the innovation and modern fields are immediately turned into new modes. Such a change continues at phenomenal speed. Results of the change in a general sense changed the current innovation and industry. When IoT is applied to a field, the field can make sure about scholarly execution. IoT empowers a framework itself to lead scholarly judgment and the executives, with human mediations or organization. The presentation of IoT permits objects in genuine world to settle on versatile choices and do scholarly activities, which have been made conceivable just by people.

For IoT, the parts of organizations are significant. Organization advancements utilized in IoT steadily what's more, mentally communicate gathered information at any unfavorable conditions. IoT can be likewise utilized as an instrument to impart or trade data, in that it can mentally keep on send information and keep up organizations and it gives setting data by which settings in genuine world can be distantly perceived. In this manner, IoT can be utilized as a specialized instrument in condition in which correspondence isn't effortlessly executed or during the time spent works portrayed by troublesome correspondence. Moreover, it tends to be additionally utilized for individuals with open issues.

Home Appliance Control
The above Fig. 5 is the yield for IoT based home apparatuses control utilizing retina development. The IR transmitter is utilized to move the developments of eyeball sensor to the IR collector, at that point the home machines are constrained by utilizing the hand-off circuit. IoT is the most focal innovation that drives the fourth modern upset.

Fig. 5. Home appliances control

5 Conclusion

In this way a knowledge control framework utilizing retina development is intended for physically incapacitated individuals. The venture controls the IoT based wheelchair development and the home apparatuses utilizing the retina development. Computerized wheel seat can be used to support physically incapacitated persons, particularly the persons who are not ready to move. The framework was effectively executed to move the wheel seat Left, Right, Forward, Backward or Stay similarly situated.

Future Work
The future work may be designed to control more home appliances. Health monitoring along with GPS transmission added to the project to intimate the attenders in case of any emergency. The control through retina control shall be extended that even mobile phones are accessed by the retina movement itself. The wheelchairs shall be made compactable so that it shall be handy and can be used whenever needed.

References

1. Topal, C., et al.: A wearable head-mounted sensor-based apparatus for eye tracking applications. In: IEEE Conference on Virtual Environments, Human-Computer Interfaces and Measurement Systems, pp. 136–139 (2008)
2. Lu, Z., Chen, X., et al.: A hand gesture recognition framework and wearable gesture-interaction prototype for mobile devices. IEEE Trans. Hum. Mach. Syst. **44**, 293–299 (2014)
3. Srihari, K., et al.: Automatic battery replacement of robot. Adv. Nat. Appl. Sci. **9**, 33–38 (2015)
4. Rakhi Kalantri, A., Chitre, D.K.: Automatic wheelchair using recognition. Int. J. Eng. Adv. Tech. **2**, 6 (2013)

5. Vetrivelan, P., et al.: A neural network based automatic crop monitoring robot for agriculture. In: The IoT and the Next Revolutions Automating the World, pp. 203–212. IGI Global, Hershey (2019)

6. Santhi, S., Udayakumar, E., Gowthaman, T.: SOS emergency ad hoc wireless network. In: Anandakumar, H., Arulmurugan, R., Onn, C.C. (eds.) Computational Intelligence and Sustainable Systems. EICC, pp. 227–234. Springer, Cham (2019). https://doi.org/10.1007/978-3-030-02674-5_15

7. Megalingam, R.K., et al.: Automated voice based home navigation system for the elderly and the physically challenged. In: International Conference on Advanced Communication Technology (2011)

8. Kanagaraj, T., et al.: Foot pressure measurement by using ATMEGA 164 microcontroller. Adv. Nat. Appl. Sci. **10**, 224–228 (2016)

9. Murarka, A., et al.: Detecting obstacles & drop-offs stereo and motion cues for safe local motion. In: IEEE International Conference on Intelligent Robots and Systems (2008)

10. Wang, J., Chuang, F.: An accelerometer-based digital pen with a trajectory recognition Algo for handwritten digit & gesture recognition. IEEE Trans. Indust. Electron. **59**, 2998–3007 (2012)

11. Srihari, K., et al.: Automatic battery replacement of robot. Adv. Nat. Appl. Sci. **9**(7), 33–38 (2015)

12. Vetrivelan, P., et al.: Design of smart surveillance security system based on wireless sensor network. Int. J. Res. Stud. Sci. Eng. Technol. **4**(5), 23–26 (2017)

13. Prakash, N., et al.: Arduino based traffic congestion control with automatic signal clearance for emergency vehicles and stolen vehicle detection. In: Proceedings of IEEE International Conference on Computing, Communication and Informatics (ICCCI 2020), Coimbatore (2020)

14. Srihari, K., Sakthivel, V., Reddy, G.V.K., Subhasree, S., Sankavi, P., Udayakumar, E.: Implementation of Alexa-based intelligent voice response system for smart campus. In: Saini, H.S., Srinivas, T., Vinod Kumar, D.M., Chandragupta Mauryan, K.S. (eds.) Innovations in Electrical and Electronics Engineering. LNEE, vol. 626, pp. 849–855. Springer, Singapore (2020). https://doi.org/10.1007/978-981-15-2256-7_80

15. Prakash, N., Udayakumar, E., Kumareshan, N., Gowrishankar, R.: GSM-based design and implementation of women safety device using Internet of Things. In: Peter, J.D., Fernandes, S.L., Alavi, A.H. (eds.) Intelligence in Big Data Technologies—Beyond the Hype. AISC, vol. 1167, pp. 169–176. Springer, Singapore (2021). https://doi.org/10.1007/978-981-15-5285-4_16

16. Singh, H.R., et al.: Design & develop of voice/joystick speed micro control based integent motorised wheelchair. In: IEEE Tencon, pp. 1573–1576 (1999)

17. Udayakumar, E., Kanagaraj, T., Venkata Koti Reddy, G., Srihari, K., Chandragandhi, S.: Control of home appliances and projector by smart application using SEAP Protocol. In: Das, H., Pattnaik, P.K., Rautaray, S.S., Li, K.-C. (eds.) Progress in Computing, Analytics and Networking. AISC, vol. 1119, pp. 603–610. Springer, Singapore (2020). https://doi.org/10.1007/978-981-15-2414-1_60

18. Udayakumar, E., Ramesh, C., Yogeshwaran, K., Tamilselvan, S., Srihari, K.: An enhanced face and iris recognition-based new generation security system. In: Singh, P.K., Pawłowski, W., Tanwar, S., Kumar, N., Rodrigues, J.J.P.C., Obaidat, M.S. (eds.) Proceedings of First International Conference on Computing, Communications, and Cyber-Security (IC4S 2019). LNNS, vol. 121, pp. 845–855. Springer, Singapore (2020). https://doi.org/10.1007/978-981-15-3369-3_62

19. Udayakumar, E., Tamilselvan, S., Srihari, K., Venkata Koti Reddy, G., Chandragandhi, S.: A smart industrial pollution detection and monitoring using Internet of Things (IoT). In: Singh, P.K., Sood, S., Kumar, Y., Paprzycki, M., Pljonkin, A., Hong, W.-C. (eds.) FTNCT 2019. CCIS, vol. 1206, pp. 233–242. Springer, Singapore (2020). https://doi.org/10.1007/978-981-15-4451-4_18

20. Natarajan, T., Kartheeka, S.: Intelligent control systems for physically disabled and elderly people for indoor navigation. Int. J. Res. Appl. Sci. Eng. Technol. **2**, 198–205 (2014)

21. Mtshali, P., Khubisa, F.: A smart home appliance control system for physically disabled people. In: Proceedings of the 2019 Conference on Information Communications Technology and Society (ICTAS), Durban, South Africa, pp. 1–5 (2019)

22. Hartman, A., Nandikolla, V.K.: Human-machine interface for a smart wheelchair. J. Robot. **2019**, 1–11 (2019)

23. Zhang, Y., Zhang, J., Luo, Y.: A novel intelligent wheelchair control system based on hand gesture recognition. In: 2011 IEEE/ICME International Conference on Complex Medical Engineering, Harbin Heilongjiang, pp. 334–339 (2011)

24. Gagan, J.: IOT based system for person with physical disability. Int. J. Innov. Res. Electr. Electron. Instrum. Control Eng. **4**(Special Issue 2), 157–160 (2016)

25. Karthik Narayanan, M., et al.: Intelligent home monitoring using IoT for physically challenged. Int. Res. J. Eng. Technol. **06**(03) (2019)

26. Suh, D., et al.: An urgent communication way of utilizing IOT sensor for the disabled. Int. J. Control Autom. **11**(3), 23–34 (2018)

27. Gupta, A.K., Johari, R.: IOT based electrical device surveillance and control system. In: Proceedings of the 4th International Conference on Internet of Things: Smart Innovation and Usages (IoT-SIU), Ghaziabad, India, pp. 1–5 (2019)

28. Prakash, N., et al.: Design and development of Android based Plant disease detection using Arduino. In: Proceedings of the 7th International Conference on Smart Structures and Systems (ICSSS), India, 2020, pp. 1–6 (2020)

29. Adhav, V., et al.: An IoT based monitoring and control system for environmental conditions and safety in home. Int. J. Eng. Develop. Res. **4**(4) (2016)

30. Tamilselvan, S., et al.: Development of Artificial Intelligence based assessment writing robot for disable people. In: 7th International Conference on Smart Structures and Systems (ICSSS), India, pp. 1–6 (2020)

31. Ghazal, B., Khatib, K.: Smart home automation system for elderly and handicapped people using XBee. Int. J. Smart Home **9**, 203–210 (2015)

32. Srihari, K., et al.: An innovative approach for face recognition using raspberry Pi. Artif. Intell. Evol. **1**(2), 103–108 (2020)

Role of Classification Model with Fuzzy Model to Predict Covid-19: A Comparative Study

Laxmi Verma Arya[✉] and Preetvanti Singh

Faculty of Science, Dayalbagh Educational Institute, Dayalbagh, Agra, India

Abstract. The ongoing Coronavirus pandemic is the infectious disease brought about by the latest discovered coronavirus, and is affecting many countries globally. At the present time it is difficult to test everybody globally so a model is developed in this paper that can help in predicting the risk of coronavirus. A decision tree is constructed for this purpose based on certain attributes like fever, dry cough, tiredness, difficulty to breath, and chest pain; and is compared using various other methods. Classification Functions are used for the prediction and the results are compared based on accuracy. It was observed that Multilayer Perceptron classifier achieved the highest accuracy of 95.31%, however the generated tree using J48 achieved same accuracy (90.63%) as that of LMT & Logistic classifiers. Rules generated by Decision tree are then used in the Fuzzy Inference System using MATLAB to give predictions related to the disease risk.

Keywords: Novel coronavirus · J48 · Classification · Decision tree · Fuzzy inference system · Covid-19

1 Introduction

COVID is an infection that causes an infection in the upper throat or sinuses, nose. In 2019 World Health Organization recognized a new type of coronavirus, SARS-CoV-2, that causes extreme illnesses like Middle East respiratory syndrome and sudden acute respiratory syndrome. A novel coronavirus was later recognized in Wuhan (China) that quickly spreads bringing scourge to different nations all through the world. The World Health Organization assigned this COVID-19 in 2020 [1]. COVID-19 has been marked as a general wellbeing crisis of global concern, and the pestilence bends are as yet on the ascent [24]. In all ages, including children, Infection has been reported. Most of the infections are mild, giving a flu-like sickness. The most normal sign at disease beginning is weakness-70%, fever-99%, myalgia-44%, dry cough-60%, and dyspnea [18–20]. Fewer normal signs are dizziness, headache, diarrhea, vomiting and nausea [21]. Dyspnea, pharyngeal agony, abdominal pain, anorexia, and dizziness are symptoms to be available in patients with extreme sicknesses [19]. Additionally, older patients have basic chronicity as well as hypertension, cardiovascular illness, cerebrovascular sickness, and diabetes, are bound to have unfavorable results (Fig. 1).

© Springer Nature Switzerland AG 2021
R. Agrawal et al. (Eds.): ICCEDE 2020, CCIS 1436, pp. 141–151, 2021.
https://doi.org/10.1007/978-3-030-84842-2_11

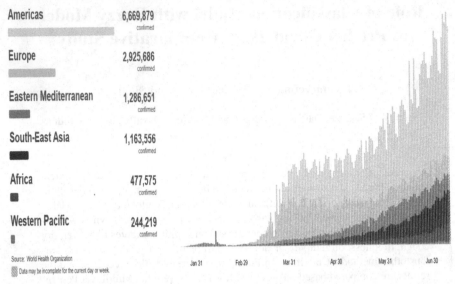

Fig. 1. Cumulative global case counts (Source: https://covid19.who.int)

The main reason for this spread is unawareness. Methods are required to make people aware of the symptoms of COVID-19. Artificial intelligence (AI) and data mining are some of the approaches to develop such methods [2].

Due to COVID-19 pandemic, there is a great impact on the global economy, as a large number of workers, organizations, and businesses around the globe become reliant on computerized infrastructure i.e. corporations and authorities around the globe have no other alternative than giving adaptable working conditions including work from home during the COVID-19 pandemic. Currently, uncommon digital reliance, secure and safe access to online infrastructure and services are critical, as we are seeing a rise in cybercriminal action attempting to misuse this crisis. Some sectors, such as health, retail, and logistics, have had greater importance, thus, attracted more cyber-attacks than usual. Cyber security challenges and solutions based on Data mining and machine learning algorithms should be investigated mainly in the health, retail, and logistics sectors.

2   Related Work

Randhawa et al. recognized a characteristic COVID-19 infection genomic signature and utilized it along with an AI based arrangement free methodology for characterization of entire COVID-19 infection genomes [3]. Naudé talked about regions where AI can add to the battle against COVID-19 [4]. Shi et al. proposed an infection Size Aware Random Forest method for Large-Scale Screening of COVID-19 using Infection Size-Aware Classification [5]. Ardabili et al. presented a paper to foresee the COVID-19 flare-up and perform a comparative analysis based on soft computing, and machine learning models [6]. Pandey et al. analyzed the outbreak of coronavirus disease using SEIR model and Regression model and predicted the number of instances for the following fourteen days for India till 30th March 2020 [7].

One of the approaches for this is to develop a method for predicting corona on the basis of COVID-19 un-obvious symptoms. Classification technique aims to predict precisely the objective class for each instance of the dataset dependent on a preparation set. Barstugan et al. implemented detection process using machine learning methods on abdominal Computed Tomography images of Coronavirus [8]. Narin et al. suggested three distinctive convolutional neural organization based models for the recognition of Covid pneumonia tainted patient utilizing lung X-beam radiographs [9].

Ozkaya proposed a method to detect COVID-19 in early phase using feature fusion and ranking method with Support Vector Machine [10]. Samuel et al. provided a methodological outline of two machine learning classification strategies, with regards to the printed investigation, and compared their adequacy in characterizing Coronavirus Tweets of varying lengths [11]. Ghoshal et al. proposed a model to assess the analysis vulnerability in coronavirus forecast dependent on Bayesian Convolutional Neural organization [13]. Cohen et al. obtained 70 chest X-beam pictures of coronavirus patients from coronavirus dataset and deduced that Bayesian derivation enhance the identification precision of VGG16 framework [14].

Wang et al. proposed a deep convolutional neural network-based model to detect COVID-19 instance using X-beam picture [15]. Painuli et al. developed a Fuzzy Rule Based model to predict COVID-19 [16]. Dhiman et al. developed a fuzzy inference system for diagnosing the COVID-19 illness based on various input factors [17]. In this paper first develops a decision tree to predict the class label for COVID-19 dependent on the manifestations, and compares the outcomes using Weka, and then develop a Fuzzy model to predict covid-19 disease risk.

3 Material and Methods

Classification technique, a supervised learning method, allots things in an assortment to all the objective classifications. For solving both regression and classification problems decision tree is a supervised machine learning procedure. It helps in distinguishing the relationship among the information that focuses on a dataset by building tree structures. Decision trees are developed as a top-to-down organized framework in the divide-and-conquer manner. Decision Tree is non-parametric, various leveled arrangement technique that predicts class enrollment by recursively apportioning an informational collection into more modest developments or more homogeneous subsets [12].

Continuous as well as discrete parameters are classified by C4.5 which is a statistical classifier. It can effortlessly deal with datasets that have parameters having different costs as well as with missing parameters.

In this study, the first C4.5 algorithm is hired for the building of the Decision Tree. It works on a divide and conquers mechanism to extend the Decision Tree by iteratively deciding the parameters that finest split the data into many similar classes. Based on the rules generated by decision tree a fuzzy inference system is created. The framework of the developed model is appeared in Fig. 2.

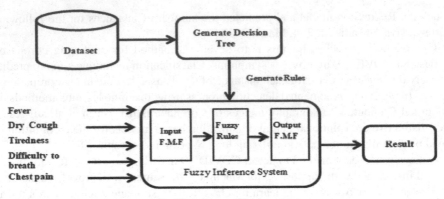

Fig. 2. Suggested framework

Decision tree is created to predict the risk of coronavirus disease into four classes; Covid_Yes, Covid_risk_high, Covid_No, Covid_risk_low. This classification is based on the five input parameters; fever, dry cough, tiredness, difficulty to breath, and chest pain. Figure 3 shows the generated Decision Tree.

Every way from the root to a leaf is a rule. In decision tree Entropy is a proportion of the uncertainty associated with a arbitrary variable. The original entropy of the dataset K, is computed by:

$$H[K] = -\sum_{j=1}^{[C]} P(C_j) log_2 P(C_j)$$

Where, C is the set of desired class.

The knowledge expressed by human is well realized by fuzzy Inference systems, thus there is a possibility to implement the human expertise and knowledge. Based on the generated rules, Fuzzy Inference System is generated as illustrated in Fig. 4.

Membership function is used to represent the degree of truth in fuzzy logic as shown in Fig. 5. A pictorial portrayal of fuzzy set is possible with the help of membership functions. In the representation the universe of discourse and degree of membership between [0,1]. Symptoms of the disease are used as the inputs to design the membership functions. Trapezoidal Membership Function is used for defining membership functions within the range (0–1) [23]. The Trapezoidal bend is an element of a vector, x, and relies upon four scalar boundaries a, b, c, and d.

Mathematical representation of Trapezoidal membership functions is:

$$\mu_B(X) = \begin{cases} 0 & (x < a) \text{ or } (x > d) \\ \frac{x-a}{b-a} & a \le x \le b \\ 1 & b \le x \le c \\ \frac{d-x}{d-c} & b \le x \le c \end{cases}$$

The parameters are characterized by a lower cutoff a, a maximum cutoff d, a lower support cutoff b, and an upper help cutoff c, where a < b < c < d.

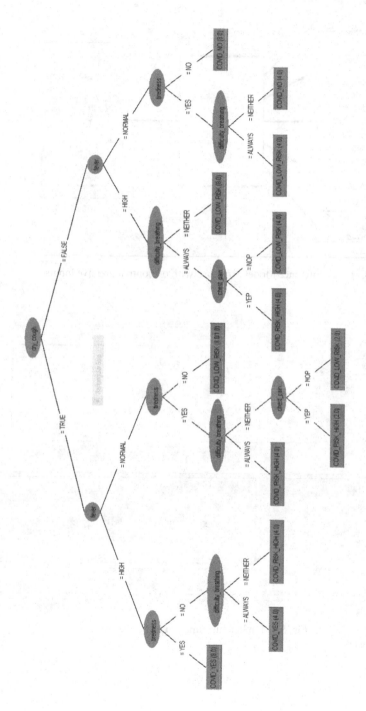

Fig. 3. Constructed Decision Tree by the C4.5 method for the prediction of coronavirus disease risk.

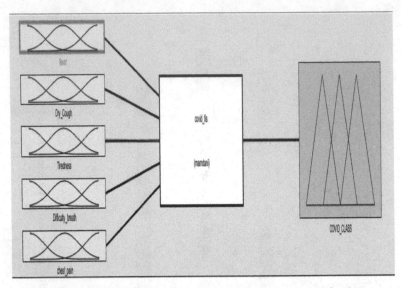

Fig. 4. Fuzzy Inference Model Structure with one output and five inputs.

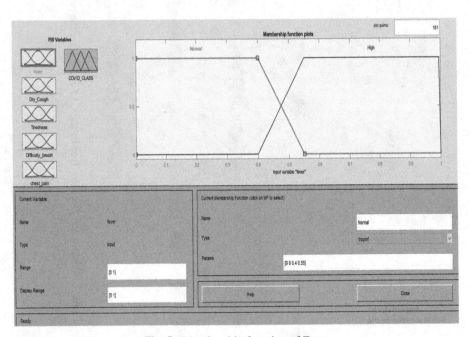

Fig. 5. Membership function of Fever.

4 Result

Weka Tool is used to create Decision Tree whereas MATLAB is used to implement the proposed Fuzzy model. Input data set consists of fever, tiredness, dry cough, difficulty to breathe and chest pain [18–20]. The output consists of four classes covid_yes, covid_risk_high, covid_risk_low, covid_no. For the prediction in Weka Hoeffding Tree, Decision Stump, LMT, REP Tree, J48, Random Tree, Random Forest, Classification Functions, and Bayes classifiers are used. And compare the results on the basis of accuracy. The Multilayer Perceptron classifier accomplished the highest precision at 95.31%, Rndom Forest achieved 93.75% and J48 LMT & Logistic classifier achieved the same accuracy which is 90.63% (Fig. 6).

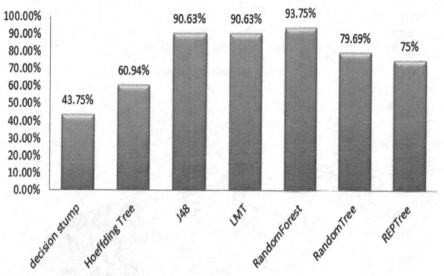

Fig. 6. Correctly classified instances of coronavirus disease based on different classification algorithms.

Figure 7 shows the possible symptoms of the coronavirus on rule viewer with the description of the rules. It is the complete roadmap of inference process defined for the prediction of covid-19 risk. This is important part of the MATLAB tool as this viewer shows how individual membership function diagram affects the output.

Figure 8 shows the representation in 3D form as a rule surface performed in MATLAB on Dry_cough and fever. Membership function of this surface shows that if someone is suffering from fever and have dry cough then the possibility of being infected by coronavirus is positive.

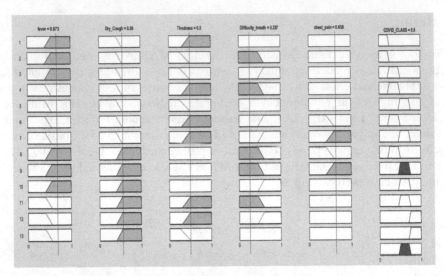

Fig. 7. Fuzzy inference system output.

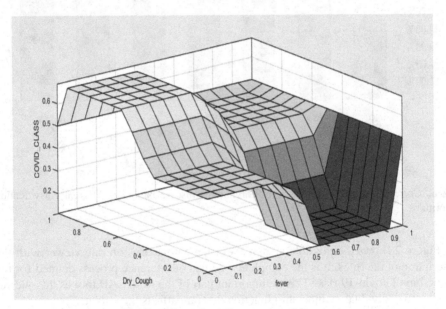

Fig. 8. Rule surface (dry cough and fever).

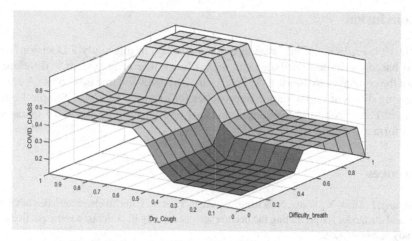

Fig. 9. Rule surface (dry cough and difficulty to breath).

Figure 9 shows the representation in 3D form as a rule surface performed in MATLAB on Dry_cough and Difficulty_breath. Membership function of this surface shows that if someone is suffering from fever and have dry cough then the possibility of being infected by coronavirus is positive.

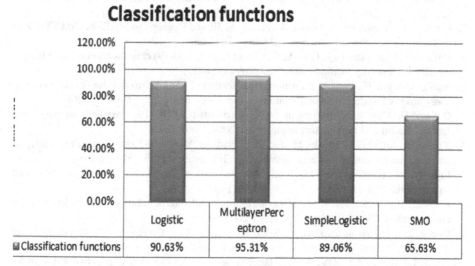

Fig. 10. Correctly classified instances of coronavirus disease based on different classification functions.

Figure 10 shows the comparison among different classification approaches for example Simple Logistic, Multilayer Perceptron, Sequential minimal optimization and Logistic on covid-19 instances.

5 Conclusion

COVID-19 is really a serious issue in the globe today. In this study a Decision Tree is created based on limited attributes and then a fuzzy inference system is developed to forecast the coronavirus disease risk. Precision of this decision tree is 90.63%. A comparison among different classification approaches for example Logistic, Simple Logistic, Multilayer Perceptron, and Sequential minimal optimization on covid-19 instances is also performed.

References

1. Ouyang, J., Shan, X., Wang, X., Zhang, X., Chen, Y., et al.: Clinical characteristics of COVID-19 and the model for predicting the occurrence of critically ill patients: a retrospective cohort study. medRxiv (2020)
2. Bullock, J., Pham, K.H., Lam, C.S.N., Luengo-Oroz, M.: Mapping the landscape of artificial intelligence applications against COVID-19. arXiv:2003.11336 (2020)
3. Randhawa, G.S., Soltysiak, M.P., El Roz, H., de Souza, C.P., Hill, K.A., Kari, L.: Machine learning using intrinsic genomic signatures for rapid classification of novel pathogens: COVID-19 case study. PLoS ONE **15**(4), e0232391 (2020)
4. Naudé, W.: Artificial Intelligence against COVID-19: an early review (2020)
5. Shi, F., et al.: Large-scale screening of covid-19 from community acquired pneumonia using infection size-aware classification. arXiv:2003.09860 (2020)
6. Ardabili, S.F., et al.: Covid-19 outbreak prediction with machine learning. SSRN 3580188 (2020)
7. Pandey, G., Chaudhary, P., Gupta, R., Pal, S.: SEIR and Regression Model based COVID-19 outbreak predictions in India. arXiv:2004.00958 (2020)
8. Barstugan, M., Ozkaya, U., Ozturk, S.: Coronavirus (covid-19) classification using ct images by machine learning methods. arXiv:2003.09424 (2020)
9. Narin, A., Kaya, C., Pamuk, Z.: Automatic detection of coronavirus disease (covid-19) using x-ray images and deep convolutional neural networks. arXiv:2003.10849 (2020)
10. Ozkaya, U., Ozturk, S., Barstugan, M.: Coronavirus (COVID-19) classification using deep features fusion and ranking technique. arXiv:2004.03698 (2020)
11. Samuel, J., Ali, G.G., Rahman, M., Esawi, E., Samuel, Y.: Covid-19 public sentiment insights and machine learning for tweets classification. Information **11**(6), 314 (2020)
12. Friedl, M.A., Brodley, C.E.: Decision tree classification of land cover from remotely sensed data. Remote Sens. Environ. **61**(3), 399–409 (1997)
13. Ghoshal, B., Tucker, A.: Estimating uncertainty and interpretability in deep learning for coronavirus (COVID-19) detection. arXiv:2003.10769 (2020)
14. Cohen, J.P., Morrison, P., Dao, L., Roth, K., Duong, T.Q., Ghassemi, M.: Covid-19 image data collection: prospective predictions are the future. arXiv:2006.11988 (2020)
15. Wang, L., Wong, A.: COVID-net: a tailored deep convolutional neural network design for detection of COVID-19 cases from chest X-ray images. arXiv:2003.09871 (2020)
16. Painuli, D., Mishra, D., Bhardwaj, S., Aggarwal, M.: Fuzzy rule based system to predict COVID19-a deadly virus. Way **3**(4), 5 (2020)
17. Dhiman, N., Sharma, M.K.: Fuzzy logic inference system for identification and prevention of coronavirus (COVID-19)
18. Bai, Y., et al.: Presumed asymptomatic carrier transmission of COVID-19. JAMA **323**(14), 1406–1407 (2020)

19. Chen, N., et al.: Epidemiological and clinical characteristics of 99 cases of 2019 novel coronavirus pneumonia in Wuhan, China: a descriptive study. Lancet **395**(10223), 507–513 (2020)
20. World Health Organization. https://www.who.int/docs/default-source/coronaviruse/clinical-management-of-novel-cov.pdf. Accessed 16 Feb 2020
21. Huang, C., et al.: Clinical features of patients infected with 2019 novel coronavirus in Wuhan, China. Lancet **395**(10223), 497–506 (2020)
22. Coronavirus COVID-19 Global Cases by Centre for Systems Science and Engineering, p. 1. Johns Hopkins University. https://gisanddata.maps.arcgis.com/apps/opsdashboard/index.html#/bda7594740fd40299423467b48e9ecf6. Accessed 13 Feb 2020
23. https://in.mathworks.com/help/fuzzy/trapmf.html
24. World Health Organization: Situation Report-24. WHO, Geneva (2020)

Author Index

Printed in the United States
by Baker & Taylor Publisher Services